THE SECRETS OF
OKINAWAN
KARATE

THE SECRETS OF OKINAWAN KARATE

Essence and Techniques

KIYOSHI ARAKAKI

KODANSHA INTERNATIONAL
Tokyo • New York • London

Master Choki Motobu practicing Naifanchi.

Master Shoshin Nagamine practicing Naifanchi.

Shihan Kiyoshi Arakaki
c/o Okinawa Karate-Do Center
153 East 4370 South
Murray, Utah 84107
U.S.A.
(801) 262-1785

NOTE: The names of modern and contemporary Japanese appear in the Western order, while those of historical figures (pre–1868) are written in the traditional order, surname preceding given name.

Photography by Kazuki Arakaki
Illustrations by Reiko Nakamura

Originally published in Japanese as *Okinawa Budo-karate no Gokui* by Fukushodo in 2000.

Distributed in the United States by Kodansha America, Inc., 575 Lexington Avenue, New York, N.Y. 10022, and in the United Kingdom and continental Europe by Kodansha Europe Ltd., 95 Aldwych, London WC2B 4JF.

Published by Kodansha International Ltd., 17-14 Otowa 1-chome, Bunkyo-ku, Tokyo 112-8652, and Kodansha America, Inc. Copyright © 2002 by Kiyoshi Arakaki and Kodansha International Ltd. All rights reserved. Printed in Japan.

ISBN 4-7700-2759-1
First edition, 2002
02 03 04 05 06 07 08 09 10   10 9 8 7 6 5 4 3 2 1

www.thejapanpage.com

PREFACE

In traditional Okinawan karate, *kata* (form) and *kumite* (fighting) were not divided. They were taught together as one art. Today karate is practiced differently. When one sees a karate tournament or visits a karate *dojo* (school), one invariably observes kata and kumite being taught separately, as if they were unrelated to each other and had little or no connection. Kata is seen as something to learn only in order to advance to a higher rank or to show off one's style in the dojo and expertise in tournaments. Practitioners and audience alike appreciate only its outside beauty and forget that it is part of a greater whole. Kata study today places the main emphasis on how to make the kata more appealing to outside observers, often discarding or forgetting its inner nature. *Karateka* (students of karate) are often more interested in the sport and exercise aspects of karate than in the mastery of karate as a science. For karate schools to survive as businesses, it has gradually become necessary to establish karate in the world of sports or for *enbu* (performance). Over time less and less emphasis has been placed on the scientific aspects of this martial art.

Karate was developed as a weaponless method of self-defense. In the eighteenth century, the invention of machinery created new jobs as well as newer and more efficient methods of accomplishing the old jobs. This new physical climate treated the human body as a tool, and the perfected body movements of karate began to be replaced. The martial arts as practiced today have been greatly influenced by Western ideas and are considered by many to be more of a sport. This emphasis has led away from an understanding of the physical culture from which it developed. Centuries ago, the ancient martial arts masters attained the perfect fusion of physical dexterity and insight into the laws of the universe. Kata nowadays is viewed as something unnecessary for kumite, and vice versa; thus the split between their integration has widened. The modernized kata and basic movements do not work in sparring competition or in fighting. Karate practitioners, who want to be strong and do well in fighting, see no connection between kata and kumite. We have forgotten that during that ancient culture of ideal physical development, kata and basics were the main emphasis in martial arts.

In this book I will explain the essence of Okinawan karate and the purpose and necessity of kata study. I will also explore *tsuki* (punching) through Naifanchi, the ultimate kata of Shuri-te and Tomari-te. I will examine the Okinawan martial art's culture of physical perfection, of which all karateka are proud.

Readers and students of karate will find in this book a perspective on karate completely different from any they have ever seen or practiced before. These observations have evolved over more than thirty years of my personal experience: being taught Okinawan karate by masters in Okinawa, fighting in full-contact karate matches, fighting Muay-Thai in Thailand, and teaching at Muso-Kai dojo. I hope that the reader will find this book rewarding and enlightening.

Kiyoshi Arakaki

CONTENTS

Chapter 1

TSUKI AND THE INNER PHYSICAL DYNAMIC SYSTEM

Figs. 1–2 Only chambering the fist and extending it is a mechanical move.

T *suki* (punching) is the core of traditional Okinawan karate. The understanding of karate's tsuki today is to stand in a wide stance, drop the
waist, chamber a fist at the waist, extend the fist from the waist straight to
the target, and use *kime* (focus) at the penetration point in order to stop the strike
at the target. You might be surprised to learn that there is no kime in traditional
Okinawan karate as a martial art, especially in the tsuki of Shuri-te. Keep this in
mind as you read this book.

Why is there no *kime*? In modern karate, you make a tight fist, chamber the fist
at the waist, and extend it from the waist (point A) toward the target (point B) as
fast as you can (figs. 1–2). This is a mechanical move that does not apply to karate
as a martial art. The laws of physics apply to everything in this universe, including
modern sports, but there is a misinterpretation of how to apply Newton's second
law of motion—F (force energy) = M (mass) × A (acceleration)—to karate. In martial arts, you must apply this law inside your body instead of outside in order to
punch or kick. This application is called the "Inner Physical Dynamic System."

Why is there this misinterpretation of how to apply Newton's law in karate?
Karate was introduced to Japan from Okinawa during Japan's modernization.
The mechanics of movement were prominent in world thought and development. These mechanics were applied to karate. As you can see in diagram 1, the
human body was viewed as a machine: the waist was an energy source and a
shoulder was rotated to execute a punch. Based on the action and reaction theory of mechanical movement, a more powerful waist rotation was needed to add
energy and speed. According to this theory, you must be born with strong muscles and natural speed and agility; otherwise you would have no chance to excel
as a martial artist. Consequently, following this line of thinking, a small person
would have no possibility of fighting and winning against a large, powerful

Diag. 1 The waist is an energy source and a shoulder is rotated to execute a punch.

Diag. 2 The tsuki of Shuri-te is like a cowboy cracking his whip.

adversary. This is an exaggeration of the truth. While strong muscles are important and it is necessary to strengthen your muscles by lifting weights, karate does not rely only on big muscles.

TSUKI THAT EXCEED THE SPEED OF SOUND

There are two karate styles in Okinawa, and these two have different methods of tsuki, or punches. One style is called Shuri-te and the other Naha-te. This book deals mainly with Shuri-te style, and from time to time compares it with Naha-te style.

In both styles, instead of simply moving a solid object (the fist) from point A to point B, you consciously increase the speed of the fist as you punch. On television and in movies you have seen a cowboy crack a whip, making a sound that helps him move cattle into an enclosure. Some cowboys even use these skills in rodeo competition. It is so natural for them that they can produce the crack without thinking. This crack that exceeds the speed of sound is a key to karate. The tsuki of Shuri-te is like this whip (diag. 2). Think of your entire body—waist, arm, wrist, and fingers—as a whip delivering a tsuki that exceeds the speed of sound. This is the key to how a small and skinny person can fight successfully against a big, muscular opponent.

In Shuri-te, the energy point is the center of the body. This body center, the waist, is like the wrist of a cowboy cracking his whip. From this point you produce energy and transfer the energy to your opponent. Using the waist rotation method, you treat your body like a hard object. However, if you think of the body as a rigid object, you lose fluidity and cannot transfer all your body's energy to your target. If you use waist rotation as the key to producing power, the result will be more like using a length of 2 x 4 rather than a whip. The weight

Figs. 3–4 Whip your waist, opposing muscles will snap it first forward, then instantaneously back.

Figs. 5–7 In Shuri-te, you must turn your arm from inside to outside.

and mass of the 2 x 4 would be powerful but would lack the speed and explosion of energy delivered by the whip. Try whipping your waist, thinking of the waist as the center of your body. Opposing muscles will snap it first forward, then instantaneously back (figs. 3–4). This should feel the same as a cowboy's wrist moving up and down as he creates a whipping motion and energy. At this point, bulky body parts like tightened muscles and stabilized joints would interfere in the transfer of this whiplike energy.

This whipping motion applies not only to the waist but also to the arm, which is part of the same body-whip. It is completely different from the tsuki of modern karate, where a tight fist travels from the waist to a target in as straight a line as possible. Tsuki should be delivered this way: a fist is cocked at one's side near the waist. The fist, arm, and elbow stay close to the body until the fist reaches the center of the body. The fist begins moving out toward the target while arm and elbow are still touching the body, extending straight to the target. Turn the fist

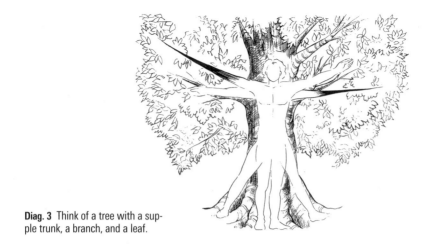

Diag. 3 Think of a tree with a supple trunk, a branch, and a leaf.

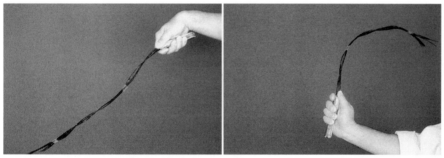

Figs. 8–9 This whipping motion applies to the waist and also to the arm.

from inside to outside as the elbow leaves the body, hitting the target at the split second of completing the fist rotation. You must turn your arm from inside to outside like a whip in order to transfer the energy created from your body (figs. 5–7). Think of a willow tree with a supple trunk, a branch, and a leaf (diag. 3). The trunk is the grip part of the whip, the branch is the main body of the whip, and the leaf is the tip of the whip. After a fist departs from the body, it must snap like a whip while turning from inside to outside.

This usage of wrist and fingers has only been passed down by oral tradition. Thus, this core concept has been lost even in Okinawa.

The energy transfer of tsuki in Okinawan karate accelerates like a rocket that has a three-level booster system to increase its speed as it departs from earth. The best way for you to transfer your energy is to become like gelatin. If your body is as hard as a rock, you just absorb energy into your body. But when you touch gelatin, it vibrates. The gelatin transfers the energy it has just received. This thought can be applied to a whip, too. A whip is flexible. Therefore, you must not tighten up any part of your body, especially the arm and hand. You never make a tight fist to hit a target. Even after hitting the target, you loosen up your hand. Only a few Okinawan karate practitioners still know about this. Actually, you never consciously tighten the fist. Just as a good whipping motion moves fluidly from the wrist to the tip of a whip, so must your tsuki move with one unbroken motion from waist to target (figs. 8–9). Instead, you simply allow the target to

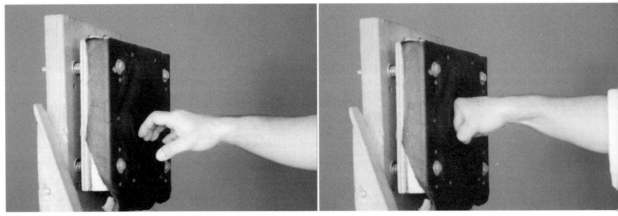

Figs. 10–11 You simply allow the target to curl the fingers into a fist.

Fig. 14 There should be no moment when you see a punch stop in the tsuki of Shuri-te.

Figs. 12–13 You can transfer 100 percent of your energy to the target without any loss.

18

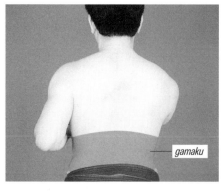
Fig. 1 The area of the back employed in *gamaku*.

curl the fingers into a fist (figs. 10–11). The only time the fist tightens is during the fraction of an instant when the fist reaches the center of the target. This is the only way to dig the fist into the target, because you can transfer 100 percent of your energy to the target without any loss (figs. 12–14). The experts, of course, hit the target with their knuckles at a 90-degree angle, and they are able to change the wrist angle instinctively to optimize contact with the target.

The tsuki of Shuri-te will always quiver because the whipping motion of the body creates energy and transfers energy completely. If a whip does not quiver, it is not a whip, it is a stick. If your body is like a stick, you destroy the speed of the tsuki. If you shake and whip the arm, the arm will relax naturally after striking and transferring energy to the target. There should be no moment when you see a punch stop in the tsuki of Shuri-te. Contrast this with modern karate, which uses the action-reaction method of pulling back the left hand to the waist so as to send energy into the right hand punch, much like a set of mechanical pistons.

When those karate practitioners who understood and performed the essence of karate as a martial art began to migrate from Okinawa to Japan and introduce karate, there were not enough of them to teach properly. They tried to teach karate to Japanese who did not have an understanding of karate by using pictures which only showed frozen moments of karate movement. This was no more successful than teaching a sports novice how to play football by using a few photos and limited instruction. As a result, the Japanese misinterpreted the Inner Physical Dynamic System of karate as being based on mechanical engineering. Thus, the essence of the original was lost.

GAMAKU AND TENDON CANCELLATION

The next technique is called *gamaku* in Okinawan dialect. *Gamaku* is a dying word even in Okinawa. Picture the muscles between the lower ribs and the hip joint. Just behind the front muscle that attaches to the hip joint is the muscle you want to isolate as you learn to use *gamaku*. The moment a fist reaches a target, you employ *gamaku* so as to rapidly contract but not tighten the muscles between the lower ribs and sacrum. *Gamaku* will put extra weight behind your tsuki and help stabilize your position, so when you hit a target, you will not be pushed back by a rebound from your own tsuki (fig. 1). Please understand: employing *gamaku* does not mean tightening up your body to protect yourself.

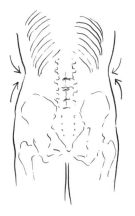

Diag. 1 When you use *gamaku*, the muscles between the lower ribs and hip joint are rapidly contracted.

Diags. 2–3 This weight feels like a balloon full of water.

To understand using *gamaku*, imagine a balloon filled with water. Put that balloon in the middle of a hand towel which you are holding at each end. Because of its weight, the balloon will pull down the towel and increase the tension of the towel. The position of the balloon in the towel is the sacrum and the ends of the towel are the ribs (diags. 1–3). Be sure that this weight feels like a balloon full of water and not a solid object like a metal ball.

The traditional Okinawan karate practitioners exercised with "tendon cancellation" to achieve tsuki with the ultimate speed and power. This exercise helps your arm become like a whip so you can transfer energy smoothly from your body to the target.

Here is the exercise to make your arm become a whip. Stand in *kiba-dachi* (horse stance, figs. 2–3). Bring the elbows up to shoulder height in front of you, arms parallel to the floor, resting both hands just above your shoulders (fig. 4). Without changing the position of the elbows, whip the fists forward as if executing a back knuckle punch, striking to the front with full strength (figs. 5–6). At the moment you reach full extension, the arms must bend a little more than 180 degrees so as to get a good stretch (figs. 7–8). You may also practice this exercise by crossing your hands in front of the chin, then extending the arms down to your sides, again extending arms to just over 180 degrees (figs. 9–10). Practice this 100 to 500 times a day to stretch and strengthen the arm muscles. It requires time and careful practice to develop this whiplike arm, because there is a tendency to overextend the elbows. Because of the fear of overextension, you must take care as you stretch these arm muscles. Begin slowly with only a few repetitions, then increase little by little daily to get used to it without causing injury.

Figs. 2–3 Stand in *kiba-dachi* (horse stance).

Fig. 4 Bring the elbows up to shoulder height, arms parallel to the floor, resting both hands just above your shoulders.

Figs. 5–6 Whip the fists forward as if executing a back knuckle punch.

Figs. 7–8 The arms must bend a little more than 180 degrees.

Figs. 9–10 You may extend arms to just over 180 degrees.

Fig. 11 Most of the time, a judge will think you are using an open hand.

Fig. 12 Jamming or breaking the fingers can occur in a full-contact tournament or a real fight.

Fig. 13 Most full-contact practitioners make a fully closed, tight fist before beginning to deliver a punch.

Some people might think that this tsuki cannot be used for a tournament. In a point-style tournament, it is hard for judges to see the motion of a tsuki that makes contact with the opponent because the motion is so small and the tsuki travels in such a tiny moment of time. Most of the time a judge will think you are hitting the opponent with an open hand (fig. 11). Full-contact practitioners think you cannot use this punch in a tournament or a real fight because jamming or breaking the fingers can occur if you make a relaxed hand with a half-open fist while blocking your opponent's punches and kicks (fig. 12). Most full-contact practitioners make a fully closed, tight fist before beginning to deliver a punch (fig. 13).

Figs. 14–15 Boxers not only protect their hands, but also use a half-open hand or relaxed fist.

Fig. 1 The tsuki of Naha-te is delivered by stabilizing the lower body momentarily, then employing *chinkuchi*.

That explains an advantage found in boxing, because boxers wrap bandages around their hands. The boxer not only protects his knuckles but also uses Shuri-te's half-open hand to make a relaxed fist (figs. 14–15). Because of the bandages, he cannot make a tightly closed fist. Therefore, his arm as well as fist muscles are relaxed and he does not lose speed and power.

DELIVERING TSUKI USING MUSCLE CONTRACTION

Here is the comparison of Naha-te with Shuri-te. The tsuki of Naha-te is delivered by fixing the lower body momentarily, then employing *chinkuchi* (fig. 1),

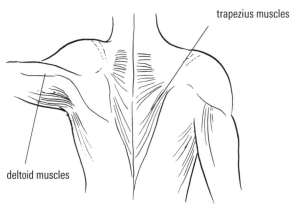

trapezius muscles

deltoid muscles

Diag. 1 When you punch, you contract the deltoid and trapezius muscles.

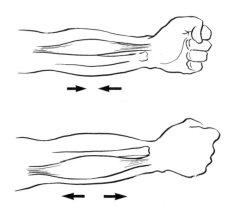

Diags. 2–3 If you contract the pronator and quadratus forearm muscles on the palm side, the supinator on the backhand side of the arm will extend.

unlike Shuri-te's tsuki which shakes and snaps the upper and lower body like a whip. *Chinkuchi* is one of the techniques of the Inner Physical Dynamic System. Literally translated, it means "one-inch power," which is the same as Bruce Lee's famous "one-inch punch." This refers to tsuki produced even though there is almost no distance between the fist and the target. How can this be accomplished? When you punch, you contract the deltoid and trapezius muscles to create the punching motion (diag. 1). With this method, you can punch while your arm is bent (figs. 2–3). In order to understand how to extend a fist to a target by contracting the muscles, take a look at your forearm. If you contract the pronator and quadratus forearm muscles on the palm side, the supinator on the backhand side of the arm will extend. This move pushes your knuckles forward (diags. 2–3). Naha-te's *Sanchin* kata employs this contraction muscle movement (figs. 4–5).

Chinkuchi is performed according to Newton's law of F = MA. You perform this within your body instead of outside (as in propelling a fist toward a target). Therefore, this tsuki can produce incredible power and lightning speed at its initiation, but since power is generated by muscle contraction, this tsuki will

Figs. 2–3 You can punch while your arm is bent.

Figs. 4–5 Naha-te's unique *Sanchin* kata.

Figs. 6–7 This tsuki can produce incredible power and lightning speed at its initiation.

Figs. 8–9 In bare-knuckled, full-contact tournaments, karate practitioners use this Naha-te style tsuki.

Figs. 10–11 A kata called *Seishan*.

Fig. 12 The tsuki of Mas Oyama (1923–1994 A.D.), the founder of Kyokushin karate (see p. 68). He employs *chinkuchi* of Goju-ryu.

Figs. 13–14 When the head receives a blow, the person is knocked out.

always be slower than Shuri-te's (figs. 6–7). The old karate masters who had the fastest tsuki were all expert in the Shuri-te style.

The advantage of Naha-te's tsuki is that your body will be solid, as the muscles are always tightened except during the split second when your fist connects with the target. Also, your opponent's kicks and punches will rebound from your solid muscles. Therefore, in bare-knuckled, full-contact tournaments, karate practitioners use this Naha-te style tsuki (figs. 8–9).

Shuri-te's Inner Physical Dynamic System offers a technique that cancels out the opponent's punches and kicks. Shuri-te students practice a kata called *Seishan* to learn how to protect against attack by using a relaxed body (figs. 10–11). Muso-Kai karate practitioners learn this Dynamic System technique after they learn the *Sanchin* kata's body contraction technique.

Once you understand the difference between the tsuki of Shuri-te and Naha-te, you must choose which punch is appropriate for which target. Shuri-te's tsuki is best applied to a target like the head, which does not have muscles to

Figs. 15–16 Naha-te's tsuki is ineffective as a strike to the head.

protect itself. When the head receives a blow, the brain reverberates within the skull and the person is knocked out (figs. 13–14). When this punch is used in a fight, whoever has the speediest and most accurate punch to his opponent's head will win the fight. It is okay to use this tsuki to the body, but it is most effectively used in a sport like boxing, where the head is the main target. But there is a disadvantage to this tsuki. Your body can only handle the reverberation shock from this full-strength punch about four or five times, because it can give tremendous damage to your body by loosening and whipping the muscles.

On the other hand, if you choose Naha-te's punch, your target should be a bigger, solid-mass object like the body (figs. 17–18). If you use this tsuki on a flexible target like the head, it is not as effective, because the head will wobble and not absorb the full impact of the strike (fig. 15–16).

The defining raison d'être of karate is that you must be able to fight empty-handed against a person or persons who have weapons. No matter how bulky and strong your muscles are, they will not stop the slice of a sword. Long ago, the Japanese conquered Okinawa and placed severe restrictions on the use of weapons by the Okinawan people. The Okinawans secretly developed karate

Figs. 17–18 Naha-te's tsuki is applied to the body.

techniques, using their bare hands to protect themselves from swords. Using their weapons inside their homes and maintaining absolute secrecy, they practiced avoiding the sword and striking back with one tsuki or *keri* (kick). Shuri-te's style of karate was the best to fight against weapon-wielding opponents because of its speed and power (figs. 19–20). The old Okinawan masters said, "Shuri-te is Okinawa's karate." The term "one shot to kill" derived from Shuri-te karate. They had to escape from attacks by weapons and kill opponents with one "shot" because there was no second chance to survive a fight (figs. 21–22). It was literally a life or death situation. There could be no tie, and second place was death.

The real fights of the old Okinawan people were not like the karate fights depicted on television or in movies. One had to dispatch his opponent as quickly and efficiently as possible. Karate was born and developed in very real fights. Traditional karate uses grabbing, throwing, and tackling (figs. 23–24). But one of the results of the Industrial Revolution is that karate has gradually evolved into a sport. Fighters spar within a limited area while keeping a tournament-approved *maai* (distance) between each other. In a real fight, of course, there is no area limit and no set *maai*.

Figs. 19–20 Okinawan people had to escape from attacks by weapons and kill opponents with one "shot."

Figs. 21–22 Shuri-te's style was developed because it was the best to use against weapon-wielding opponents.

Figs. 23–24 Traditional karate uses grabbing, throwing, and tackling.

Diags. 4–5 Practicing Shuri-te tsuki and Naha-te tsuki concurrently would be like a baseball pitcher throwing overhand and underhand in one game at full strength.

Figs. 25–26 You need to pierce a target. You do not need to hit it.

There is one thing you should never do. Okinawan masters always cautioned their students never to practice Shuri-te tsuki and Naha-te tsuki concurrently, especially while they were novice karateka. This would be like a baseball pitcher throwing overhand and underhand in one game at full strength. The pitcher would definitely destroy his shoulder (diags. 4–5). I am a living example of this. When I was young, it was one of my goals to master these two tsuki. I practiced hard and eventually injured my right shoulder, requiring major surgery. I do not want you to make the same mistake. Learn from my mistake. Fortunately, however, through this hard practice I found out one thing. If you master the principle of employing *chinkuchi* in either Shuri-te or Naha-te, you can apply this principle to the other style's punch. If you reach this level, you do not need to hit a target. The only thing you need to do is to pierce a target with your fist (figs. 25–26).

Figs. 1–2 Chinese Kung-fu's technique relies on circular motion.

Fig. 3 Japanese martial arts with respect to sword fighting are based on using a straight line to make a circle.

VARIATIONS OF TSUKI

Basically, Chinese Kung-fu's technique relies on circular motion (figs. 1–2). Japanese martial arts with respect to sword fighting are based on using a straight line to make a circle. This is the ultimate thought of the Japanese martial arts (fig. 3). If you study a swordsman swinging his sword, you will notice that his arms move forward in a straight line while the end of his sword arcs in a circle toward the target. This principle is at the core of Japanese martial arts. Your arms move forward, finding the shortest distance to a target while at the same time you create maximum energy and speed by making a circular motion with the sword. This is the superior Inner Physical Dynamic System used by Okinawan karate. The tsuki we have been discussing is based on this movement.

Figs. 1–3 When you use a hook punch, think of your arm as a whip swinging from the outside.

Although this chapter deals only with tsuki, this Inner Physical Dynamic System also applies to kicks and other body moves. In a real fight, there are no rules. You have no prior information about your opponent. Therefore, you must move your body in the most effective way possible. For example, the hook punch that most people use in a real fight has the power to destroy, but it takes more time to reach a target and exposes the ribs to attack, making one vulnerable to one's opponent. So you should not use this kind of hook punch (using a circle to make a circle) in a real fight. In order to survive in real fights against weapons, Okinawan karate developed a straight-line delivery for all kinds of punches, including hooks and uppercuts.

Hook Punch

As we have said, the most commonly used hook punch will take time to reach a target. To overcome this, think of your arm as a whip swinging from the outside while your tsuki flies straight toward the target (figs. 1–3). Or use a whip-

Fig. 4 Use a whipping motion to snap your fist into the target.

Figs. 5–6 In Muso-Kai, students practice the straight hook punch, changing the direction of the big toe to change the targeting direction of the tsuki.

ping motion to snap your fist into the target (fig. 4). As you can see in the picture, when you move into the target with a straight line, snapping the wrist in a whipping motion at the last moment as you hit the target, your fist will connect with the target at a 90-degree, maximum force angle. In Muso-Kai, higher level students practice this straight hook punch, changing the direction of the big toe to change the targeting direction of the tsuki (figs. 5–6). In this manner, you are able to punch your opponent without opening up vulnerable areas of your own body. This hook punch has the same power as the more common hook punch, but greater speed. When you are very proficient with this hook punch, you will not need the energy you formerly generated by tightening your muscles, rotating your waist, and leaving your entire side open. Even from a very

Figs. 1–2 A punch upward. As the fist travels from body to target, it moves from outside inward.

Fig. 3 At the moment that the fist comes into contact with the target, it should snap outward and back again.

close position, you can knock down your opponent by only snapping your wrist.

Uppercut Punch

This is a punch upward, say, toward your opponent's chin, with your forearm first in close with your body, then departing from the body straight to the target (figs. 1–2). As the fist travels from body to target, it moves from outside inward, and then at the moment that the fist comes into contact with the target, it should snap outward and back again at lightning speed (fig. 3). Picture the dynamic energy moving along a whip: the whip first curves outward, then straightens as

Figs. 1–2 In the backhand snap punch, you never tighten up your fist until the moment of impact.

the middle of the whip points toward its target, and finally the end of the whip snaps out and back at lightning speed as all the whip's energy explodes from its tip. For this uppercut punch, you must be close to your target to decrease the straight-line distance, then whip the fist in a circular motion which connects with the target at a 90-degree angle for maximum impact. Again, you never rotate your waist to reach the target, but move straight forward into the target.

Backhand Snap Punch

Because the backhand snap punch relies almost entirely on a whipping motion, you never tighten up your fist until the moment of impact. Feel the propulsion of energy explode down your arm and all the way to your fingertips, then whip your fingers in order to create your wrist snap. Immediately after the impact, relax your hand (figs. 1–2). Your weight must be carefully balanced when you use this strike. In traditional Okinawan karate, it was a disgrace to rely only on physical strength to break boards for *enbu* (performance). Shuri-te practitioners were proud of their ability to break boards by using only a whipping motion. Again, this is the key to how a small person can overcome a larger person. They detested relying only on pure physical strength, because it would be useless in a real fight. The use of physical strength to punch or kick is based on the action-reaction theory. It takes time to respond to the opponent's attack. By using the Inner Physical Dynamic System, you can execute response techniques before an attack reaches you. This system does not have the showmanship for modern *enbu*, but it is the essence of martial arts.

Fig. 1 *Sei-ken.*

Fig. 2 *Tate-ken.*

Fig. 3 *Naname-ken.*

Other Tsuki

There are several different tsukis. The position of the fist can be horizontal, as in *sei-ken* (formal punch, palm horizontal to the floor, fig. 1); palm vertical to the floor, as in *tate-ken* (fig. 2); or at a diagonal, or oblique angle, as in *naname-ken* (fig. 3). Some styles use a vertical or diagonal position for *sei-ken*. Of course, the angle of the fist has no bearing on the essence of the martial art of karate. What does make the difference is knowing how to stab like a knife with the fist. Which angle or fist position you use depends on the distance between you and your opponent.

You now understand the concept of using the Inner Physical Dynamic System to make tsuki. The next chapter deals with how to hit a target.

IMAGINARY CENTER
OF GRAVITY

Chapter 2

A Stance That Creates Energy

Figs. 1–2 Mechanical movement that is based on the action-reaction method of creating a punch.

When using an ordinary punch, you take a big forward stance, rotate your waist while your back leg pushes into the ground, then punch out to an opponent (figs. 1–2). As explained earlier, you should not move your body in a mechanical way that is based on the action-reaction method of creating a punch. Okinawan karate uses your entire body as a whip to deliver tsuki. This principle is in all of the Japanese martial arts. Now the question is how to move your energy against your opponent by using the Inner Physical Dynamic System.

NEWTON'S LAW OF MOTION

Try this with a friend. Face each other with hands at your sides. Bring your arms slightly forward, asking your partner to grab your wrists tightly (fig. 3). Without changing your arm level, lock your elbows close in to your body. Then just walk toward him (fig. 4). Amazing! You can lift up his body (fig. 5). Some people say this is due to *ki* (life-energy or vital force). If you move forward from this position and lift your arms a little, you can make your friend fly ten feet (fig. 6)! This is called the *aiki-age*. People explain this as making the opponent fly because there is *ki* (vital energy). This is absolutely incorrect! As you can see from diagram 1, this is a situation where your arms control his actual center of gravity (CG) because you adjust his CG higher than his true CG and your CG, and, "Voilà!" he loses his balance. You have complete control of his balance. This is an application of Newton's second law of motion, F = MA (force equals mass times acceleration).

It may be easier to think that the opponent's body is like a big box on the floor (diag. 2). Point A is the true CG. If you push this box from one side, its true CG will shift to point B (diag. 3). Apply this theory to your friend's situation.

Fig. 3 Your partner is grabbing your wrists tightly.

Fig. 4 Without changing your arm level, lock your elbows close in to your body, then just walk toward him.

Fig. 5 Amazing! You can lift up his body.

Fig. 6 You can make him fly ten feet!

Diag. 1 Situation where your arms control his actual center of gravity.

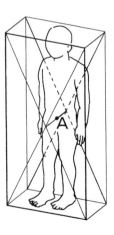

Diag. 2 The opponent's body is like a big box.

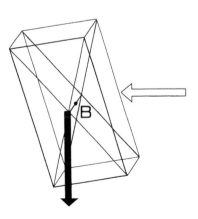

Diag. 3 If you push this box from one side, its true center of gravity will shift to point B.

When you move forward by walking with your arms in a fixed position, the true CG (point A) will be shifted to point B and will be higher than your arms' height. Because you maintain the same distance between yourself and your friend, the mass is conserved. The energy that is created by your walking is channeled in the direction that the energy is moved, which is toward your opponent. He will be forced to fall back. Point B is the best point for him to keep his balance when he is pushed; if his CG moves anywhere except point B, he loses his balance. You can now understand that the so-called Universal *Ki* is gravity, and gravity is the key for the martial artist (diag. 4). Traditional Okinawan karate uses this principle for executing tsuki. Okinawan karate recognizes this balanced CG point and the gravitational energy that is created by putting your body weight downward to create tsuki which penetrate through the target. This principle of the Inner Physical Dynamic System was an important development in all the traditional Japanese martial arts.

Diag. 4 Gravity is the key for the martial artist.

BALANCE IN UNBALANCE

First, you must understand that in order to apply Newton's second law of motion, you must train your body to find the opponent's center of gravity, as in the *aiki* throw. In karate, the technique is as follows: make a fist, then slowly fall in to your opponent (figs. 1–2). In an aiki throw, you move forward to push him up. In karate, you move forward to push him down as you fall.

Most people rotate their hips when punching, or try to keep their balance by stopping the motion of the body while falling into the target. Usually they do not fall in straight (figs. 3–4). And most likely when they do fall, they kick the ground to push into the target (fig. 5). This is wrong. Applying the Inner Physical Dynamic System to this situation, you must drop your front knee directly forward in order to fall straight in toward your opponent, and reserve the energy you have created (fig. 6). This is called "dropping the knee." While in

Fig. 1 Make a fist.

Fig. 2 You slowly fall in to your opponent.

Figs. 3–4 Usually you do not fall in straight. (This is wrong.)

Fig. 5 You kick the ground to push into the target. (This is also wrong.)

Fig. 6 You must drop your front knee directly forward in order to fall straight in toward your opponent, and reserve the energy you have created.

Figs. 7–8 Employ *gamaku* to keep your posture straight.

Figs. 9–10 Do not pull your body back too much. (This is wrong.)

this position, be sure to employ *gamaku* and to keep your elbow close to the side of your body in order to keep your posture straight (figs. 7–8). Your body should be in *hanmi* (a diagonal stance with the body at about a 45-degree angle to the attacker). When you fall from this position, your shoulder tends to fall first. Do not pull it back too much or allow your head to lean back (figs. 9–10). This motion is the same as that found in traditional Japanese swordsmanship.

When you fall, and even after the fist connects with the target, do not speed up the punch (which means you do not speed up outside your body). You accelerate inside your body using the Inner Physical Dynamic System. It will feel like you put your fist on top of the target. Of course you are in unbalance, but you are actually in balance because the target is there to stop your fall and

Fig. 11 Your body is "balance in unbalance."

Figs. 12–13 You knock him away in the next moment.

keep you in balance. Thus you can transfer the energy (which equals your weight/mass times gravity) of your fist to the target. This is called "balance in unbalance." You must use the free fall property of gravity, which pulls on your weight, generating energy. This tsuki will make the opponent's body bend in half as the result of his attempt to keep his balance, even though he has already lost his balance because of your energy. This is another example of the point B that we discussed earlier, but you cause this phenomenon to occur in his body. It only takes a split second to steal his balance, and you knock him away in the next moment (figs. 11–13). The principle of the *aiki-age* is the same as in a fist that is using Newton's second law of motion. All Japanese martial arts are based on this principle.

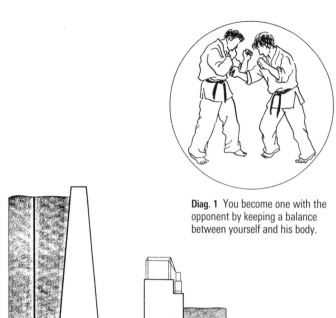

Diag. 1 You become one with the opponent by keeping a balance between yourself and his body.

Diag. 2 There is a center of gravity between this combined position.

Diag. 3 Your body is like a hydroelectric power plant. Keeping your posture straight is the same as building a dam to hold water.

IMAGINARY CENTER OF GRAVITY

The center of gravity is located about 56 percent of the body's distance above the ground for men and about 55 percent for women. This difference is because men develop about 45 percent more muscles in the front and back of their upper bodies. But there is another kind of center of gravity between you and your opponent. When you punch, you follow that invisible center of gravity and free fall with your body to create a strong punch. By doing so, it is possible to create a punch that penetrates through the opponent. You can create "one hit to kill" tsuki. This is the tsuki of Okinawan karate. First, you become one with the opponent by keeping a balance between yourself and his body (diag. 1). There is a center of gravity between this combined position, in the space between you and him (diag. 2). A key for your movement through life can also be found here. This is the principle and the basis of the science of martial arts and Muso-Kai Okinawa Karate-do, and we call this the Imaginary Center of Gravity or ICG. This principle is based on gravitational and centrifugal forces. It is interesting to note that the key to using this technique is that of going *against* gravity. This may sound like it contradicts the theory we have been talking about, but it does not. It completely obeys the laws of physics and holds the key to controlling the energy within you.

Your body is like a hydroelectric power plant. First, you build a dam to hold back the water (diag. 3). Then you use this water to power a turbine engine,

Fig. 1 Do not overstraighten into a near-perpendicular position with the floor.

Fig. 2 The upper body is often so straight that the energy is deadlocked.

producing electrical energy. I want you to understand this. Keeping your posture straight is the same as building a dam to hold water, which combines the force of what is held back with the force of gravity's pull. For another example of this, think of the Olympic ski jump. Ski jumpers try so hard to overcome gravity, yet they keep their posture straight, reserving energy and balance until the body is directed straight forward, and gravity helps them reach as far as possible. This action is the same as you will use to punch through, far beyond, your target. You must keep your posture straight, creating a dam in your body for holding back the gravitational energy. A word of caution: do not over-straighten into a near-perpendicular position with the floor or you will throw your weight back (fig. 1). Using proper straight posture, this is the most effective position from which a human can harness gravitational energy.

Unfortunately, modern karate practitioners do not understand the meaning of "straighten your posture." They think this is only for looks. A good example of this bad posture is when they do a forward *zenkutsu-dachi* (stance with front knee over the toes, back leg straight): the upper body is often so straight that the energy is deadlocked (fig. 2). It becomes static instead of kinetic. It cannot be transferred in any direction from this position without some prior movement to start the energy. This unfortunate concept occurs not only in the U.S. but also in Japan. In old Japan, there were 718 different styles of Kendo or ken-jutsu (the way of the sword). The Dai Nippon Butoku-kai (Association for the Martial Arts Virtues of Great Japan) was established in 1895 and consolidated these into one main style. This action has affected modern Japanese martial arts. The *Itto-ryu* style understood a perfectly straight stance was needed to store the gravitational

Fig. 3 A perfectly straight stance of Kendo.

energy of the stance (fig. 3). A major modern Japanese martial art which contains the gravitational control for which we are striving is Ueshiba's Aikido. Master Morihei Ueshiba realized how to use the gravitational effects that control this energy by consciously damming it until you hit a target.

TSUKI IN MUSO-KAI

The next step is to add whiplike acceleration and to free fall toward your Imaginary Center of Gravity (diags. 1–2). Start by using *tate-ken* (vertical punch) for this technique until you get used to it, then you can switch to *sei-ken* (horizontal punch).

First, bend your elbow and bring your arm up in front of you with your fist at shoulder height (fig. 2). From this position, fall into your partner until your fist makes contact with his body, using only the speed that your body allows when you fall (fig. 3). In other words, let gravity control your fall. You will free fall to the ICG. When your fist reaches your opponent, your body has reached your ICG (fig. 4). The basic stance you will use is to stand facing your opponent, lining up your ankle, knee, waist, shoulder, elbow, and wrist in one vertical plane which moves toward your target (figs. 5–6). It is interesting to note that this stance is exactly the same as the Kendo swordsmanship stance called *ma-hanmi* (figs. 7–8). Since this is a principle of both Kendo and Okinawan karate, it shows that the core concept is the same.

This book is for anyone who wishes to master karate as a martial art. So let me repeat: make sure you understand the meaning of "stand straight." You must stand so that you line up everything (your ankle, knee, waist, shoulder, elbow, and wrist) with the inside of your front foot (fig. 9). Many people, including so-called karate experts, stand with their weight outside of the front

Fig. 1 Famous Kendo master Moriji Mochida (1885–1974 A.D.) assuming the "aiming-at-the-eye" posture and demonstrating outstanding gravitational control, at Noma dojo.

Free fall

Free fall and whiplike acceleration

Diags. 1–2 Add whiplike acceleration and free fall toward your ICG.

Fig. 2 Bring your arm up in front of you with your fist at shoulder height.

Fig. 3 Use the speed that your body allows when you fall.

Fig. 4 When your fist reaches your opponent, your body has reached your ICG.

Figs. 5–6 Line up your ankle, knee, waist, shoulder, elbow, and wrist in one vertical plane.

Figs. 7–8 Kendo swordsmanship stance called *ma-hanmi*.

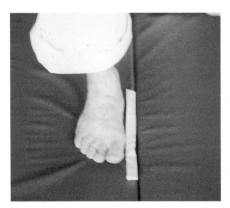

Fig. 9 You must line up everything with the inside of your front foot.

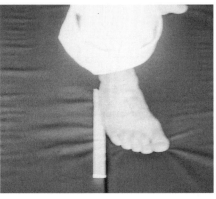

Fig. 10 You are standing with your weight outside of the front foot. (This is wrong.)

Figs. 11–12 Practice from a vertical front-leaning position with the fist slightly extended.

Fig. 13 You can make your opponent fly away even though you punch slowly.

foot. Your knee must align with the inside of the foot, or in other words, align with the big toe. If your knee aligns with the outside of the foot, your knee leans outside. As you can see in figure 10, a knee leaning to the outside will create two different vectors, thereby splitting your energy in two different directions. Your fist will be unable to strike the opponent at a 90-degree angle with full strength. When your big toe, ankle, knee, waist, shoulder, elbow, wrist, and fist are in alignment, the energy of your tsuki increases greatly because each point of these vectors is in line with the other. There is no splitting of energy in different directions. You may have heard that the big toe is important in martial arts. This is the reason. Again, make sure that you stand with all these points in alignment with the inside of your foot.

This will probably be awkward to practice at the beginning. So practice from a vertical front-leaning position with the fist slightly extended and remember to use *gamaku* (figs. 11–12). Later you will be able to whip your body and arm to transfer and accelerate the energy you create.

Remember from what you learned in Chapter 1 that you do not make a tight fist until the moment of impact. You do not consciously make a fist. Instead, the target makes the fist for you by curling in your fingers as they reach the target. Make sure to extend your arm as if stabbing with a knife. If you can do this, you will make your opponent fly away even though you punch slowly (fig. 13). After mastering this much, you simply add the physical speed of a whipping motion to increase the energy of your fist. This is the tsuki of Muso-Kai karate.

Fig. 1 A kata called Kanku. First you bring both hands up over your head.

AVOIDING *ITSUKU*

There is one thing you must understand clearly about the Imaginary Center of Gravity: the ICG must always be only imaginary. When the ICG and your body's actual center of gravity overlap, it is called *itsuku*, which means deadlocked. This is taboo for any style of martial art. A good example of *itsuku* is a gesture of surrender made by bringing both hands up over your head (fig. 1). There is a universal meaning to this: "I do not have a weapon" or "I surrender." Consider this body position relative to the laws of physics. When you assume this "surrender" position with your body perpendicular to the ground, your body is deadlocked or rooted in one place. Before you could move from this point to another, you would have to take a moment to shift your body weight and regenerate energy.

Let's use the example of a kata called Kanku, in which you must not allow your body's energy to become deadlocked, or stuck. Almost every karateka gets stuck in one spot when performing this kata. They have surrendered (fig. 4). When you perform the predecessor kata of Kanku, Kushanku, you keep your posture straight and lean forward (figs. 2–3). Remember the ski jumper? From this position, your body becomes a dam wall to store energy. Then when you punch or kick, you release this pent-up energy and transfer it to the target. It is a universal law.

This forward-leaning stance will also bring you closer to your opponent without your stepping in toward him. You gain distance by a two-dimensional move without initiating motion. Even if he sees you from the front when you make this move, he will lose the sense of the three-dimensional space you are coming from, because he only perceives you as making a two-dimensional movement within his three-dimensional world. When Kushanku evolved into Kanku (which means "look upon the sky"), the kata lost not only its name but

Figs. 2–3 The predecessor kata of Kanku, Kushanku.

Figs. 4–5 The situation of *itsuku*.

also its energy. All flow of movement stopped (figs. 4–5). People misunderstood the practical meaning of the martial arts and only considered martial arts as the combined values of spiritual and moral meaning that influenced the development of kata.

Here is an interesting thought. Suppose you are in a combat situation and are captured. (You are, of course, a master of the martial arts who understands Imaginary Center of Gravity and the Inner Physical Dynamic System.) If you assume a surrender gesture using ICG (instead of a deadlocked surrender stance), your enemy might kill you. Your enemy is probably more sensitive to any motion you make (i.e., ICG), because he has been trained for battle and he is in a life and death situation. You must use discretion in deciding when a particular technique is appropriate.

Fig. 1 *Ritsu-zen*. Imagine you are hugging a tree.

Diag. 1 You are putting your ICG in the center of your rounded arms.

STANDING ZEN

Ritsu-zen is practicing Zen while in a standing position with your arms in front of you as if you were hugging a big tree (fig. 1). This idea comes from Chinese philosophy. The belief is that you grow stronger as you become part of a big tree by holding it and receiving *ki* energy from it. I think it is good for your health to receive energy atoms emitted by the tree, but they say you can practice this by just imagining holding a tree instead of actually doing so. What is the real *Ritsu-zen*? You may understand the meaning of this after having read this far in the book. That's right. This is an example of avoiding *itsuku*. You are exercising your Imaginary Center of Gravity by putting it in the middle of a tree or in the center of your rounded arms (diag. 1).

You can move around with *Ritsu-zen*. Japanese call this *hai* (crawling) and *neri* (kneading—in this case, a slow movement of the whole body) (figs. 2–3). When you do this, consciously try to move your ICG in any direction and drop your knee in the chosen direction. Because you do this slowly, this is good for teaching your body non-deadlocked positioning. If you investigate Tai Chi Chuan as a martial art, you will see the effects of using ICG (diag. 2). When you become accomplished at *Ritsu-zen*, you will be able to place your center of gravity outside of your body (where it becomes your ICG) to create an alert, non-deadlocked position anytime, within any motion, or even if you are standing still. Now you begin to see the ultimate concept of the Inner Physical Dynamic System in traditional martial arts.

Figs. 2–3 *Neri* (kneading) and *hai* (crawling).

Diag. 2 When you practice Tai Chi Chuan very slowly, you will see the effects of using ICG.

Fig. 4 *Irimi.* You place your ICG at a 45-degree angle.

By putting your center of gravity forward and developing skills based on the recognition of the ICG, you move into your opponent at a 45-degree angle as in Aikido or Kendo practice. This is *irimi*, or the into-body position (fig. 4). *Irimi* uses an opponent's force against him by yielding; that is, instead of facing him squarely, you "yield" part of your body. Of course, this extends the opposite part of your body toward him. Placing your ICG directly in front of you or at a 45-degree angle is the basis of martial arts. But Okinawan karate's contribution to the martial arts is its unique concept of placing your ICG at a direct 90-degree angle. It is a miracle of history. Okinawan karate has developed by drawing on the Japanese and Chinese cultures and thus has made great strides in the martial arts world.

Chapter 3 | WALKING IN MARTIAL ARTS

One of the keys to martial arts is to avoid showing the initial move of your techniques, and even to try to initiate an action without any prior movement. The traditional martial arts avoided techniques that showed the initiating movement, even though some practitioners were extremely swift and agile, because those people who could move quickly relied only on their natural talent. In other words, it would be impossible for you (the not naturally talented) to win a competition with a wild cheetah (the naturally talented). Even though the cheetah is the fastest animal on the plain, this does not make him a martial artist. No matter how fast you are, speed alone is not enough. But if you want to win: (1) is there a way to originate a move quickly without telegraphing your movement when you run or dash? (2) is it possible to quickly change the direction of your movement while running? and (3) is there a way to hide your motion from your opponent while you are running? The answer to these questions is "No!" because you are running. While you are running, it is possible only to run.

Diag. 1 Tsuki using the pushing-off-the-ground energy.

In martial arts, you must be able to move in closer to your opponent without his knowledge and you must be able to change direction while you are increasing and holding your energy. It is impossible to do these actions while you are running. You will not get closer to your opponent, without his noticing, by pushing your foot off the ground in order to move forward. This enlightenment led to the birth of *ashi-sabaki* (the foot maneuvers that are characteristic of

Figs. 1–2 In sprinting, you are kicking the ground with your back foot.

martial arts). This is the main difference between sports which compete only for time and distance and martial arts which developed as the means to save one's life.

WALKING AS A TECHNIQUE

Take a look at diagram 1. This is an example of using a reaction to move forward as the back foot kicks the ground, then transferring that pushing-off-the-ground energy (Newton's third law of motion—for every action, there is an equal and opposite reaction) to your opponent. Modern karate, Judo, and Kendo use this method of producing energy. But I am sure most of you can guess that this method is wrong. This is an attempt to understand Japanese martial arts by applying Western body movement. Of course, you need to kick the ground with your back foot for certain sports, for instance, sprinting (figs. 1–2), but the goal of the 100-yard dash is completely different from karate's goal of producing maximum energy with minimum movement. As I explained earlier, you must be able to move in closer to your opponent without letting him know you are moving, and you must be able to change directions while you increase and store your energy. It is impossible to create the controlled body movement required in martial arts by running. So how can we achieve this objective? The answer is walking, because walking is a completely different body movement from running.

Here is an interesting experiment. Stand straight with your back against a wall (fig. 3). Make sure your heels, hips, elbows, and head are touching the wall. Now try to move forward like you usually walk (fig. 4). It is impossible. You feel glued to the wall. Then how can you move forward from this position? First, project

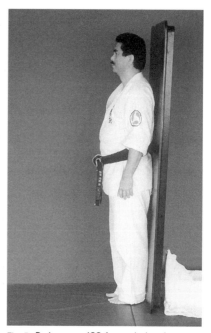

Fig. 3 Stand straight with your back against a wall.

Fig. 4 Try to move forward like you usually walk.

Fig. 5 Project your ICG forward, then lean your head forward.

Fig. 6 Drop your knee.

Fig. 7 Your body will begin to free fall.

Fig. 8 Move your other knee forward to walk.

Fig. 9 Walking is free falling to your ICG.

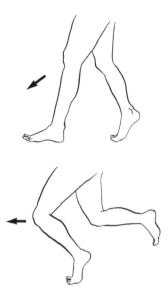

Diags. 2–3 "Walking" in martial arts is completely different from sprinting.

your Imaginary Center of Gravity forward. Then lean your head forward to that point and drop one knee (figs. 5–6). Your body will naturally begin to free fall because of gravity. As your body free falls forward, move your other knee forward to walk (figs. 7–8). This is the way we walk. Walking is free falling to your ICG (fig. 9). This concept is the essence of the techniques I explained in Chapter 2.

This is the true meaning of "walking" in martial arts. It is completely different from sprinting (diags. 2–3). Dropping your knee and letting gravity control your body's fall is the application of your martial arts techniques. This walking fulfills the three conditions that a cheetah's dash cannot. It is absolutely unnecessary to push your foot against the ground to generate the energy to move forward. Instead, simply rely on gravity's pull on your body to produce this falling energy. It is comparable to Galileo's experiment of dropping two objects from the Leaning Tower of Pisa, only you are the object being pulled by gravity (diag. 4). It is natural that if the origin of the move is free fall, you do not need to kick the ground to move forward. Therefore, your opponent cannot see the beginning of your move. This fulfills the first condition.

Then, because your leg muscles are relaxed when you use this fall, you are able to move into *hanmi* by *ashi-sabaki* foot maneuvers, changing your steps

Diag. 4 Galileo conducted an dropping experiment by dropping two objects from the Leaning Tower of Pisa.

and directions. This accomplishes the second condition of maneuvering while in motion. Keep this point in mind. When you fall, be sure to fall straight toward your ICG (figs. 10–13). If you turn your waist, the energy will go elsewhere (fig. 14). When you walk, your waist does not rotate, but you are able to walk by sliding your waist forward (fig. 15). There should be no waist rotation in Okinawan karate or Japanese Kendo. This body control produces the most effective maneuvering in martial arts. Here you see an application of making a circle with a straight line. Your movement toward the ICG between you and your opponent originates from walking, not sprinting.

In modern martial arts, the person who understood this body maneuver and used it was Morihei Ueshiba, the founder of Aikido. I will say this one more time. Transferring energy that you produce by kicking the ground is not an effective method for achieving our objectives. There is nothing more important in martial arts than using this universal law of gravity, which Ueshiba called "the essence of the Universe." This is the essential principle of Japanese martial arts' ultimate body control. Muso-Kai Okinawa Karate-do exists for this reason. We understand and practice this essential principle of the martial arts, so it has become part of us. We will now begin investigating how to fulfill the third condition of your contest with the cheetah, hiding your movements from your opponent.

CONTINUOUS STANDING

As Einstein said, physics is the study of motion in a specific place. The universe is organized according to an exact set of specific laws, or rules, and these remain constant. The study of karate also requires organization of specific rules of

Figs. 10–11 Be sure to fall toward your ICG.

Figs. 12–13 Be sure to fall straight.

Fig. 14 Don't rotate your waist.

Fig. 15 When you walk, your waist does not rotate.

Figs. 1–3 In modern karate, you first move up to an opponent, next, stabilize your position, and finally, deliver a technique. (This is wrong.)

Figs. 4–6 Modern karate uses fixed movement, not a continuous action. (This is wrong.)

movement. Modern karate believes the maneuvers are: first, move up to an opponent; next, stabilize your position; and finally, deliver a technique (figs. 1–6). But in martial arts, you must increase the energy that you produce while you are moving from point A to point B. Now, how do you increase energy while you are moving? Let's review the things we have discussed so far. Start by setting the Imaginary Center of Gravity. Next, move forward to the ICG by dropping your knee. Gravity then produces energy, caused by your movement from balance to unbalance. Finally, transfer this energy to your opponent through the selected technique. Okinawan karate discovered how to apply this universal law of movement.

Let me explain this by using a wide forward stance with the weight on the front foot. For the purpose of more easily understanding this maneuver, the person demonstrating exaggerates the moves. In other words, this is for beginners' practice. Experts can do this move as they walk. Let's practice this using *jun-zuki*

Fig. 7 *Jun-zuki*, the lunge punch.

Fig. 8 *Kakeashi-dachi*, hooked foot stance.

Fig. 9 *Musubi-dachi*, attention stance.

Fig. 10 *Musubi-dachi*, with heels together.

or *oi-zuki*, the lunge punch (fig. 7). Put your right foot forward and deliver a right punch. As you see in figure 8, the shoulders lean forward a little and you keep the weight on the balls of your feet. The ICG is in front of you and you are never stuck, or deadlocked, at any point. Depending on the ICG, you can move in any direction, even up and down, with the true *kakeashi-dachi* (hooked foot stance, fig. 8). Your opponent will go down if you execute a punch with balance in unbalance, falling into your opponent to create a new balance with him.

Next is the stance placing both heels together, called *musubi-dachi* (attention stance, figs. 9–10). This must not be the same as a military attention stance. Keep your weight on the balls of your feet with your knees just slightly bent. The only time in martial arts that you completely straighten your knees is when your body leans forward as if in a ski jump. When you stand in *musubi-dachi*, you should be poised and ready to instantaneously move one shoulder forward

to deliver a punch in the *hanmi* body position. Just as in *kakeashi-dachi*, you should be able to move in any direction with ICG, punches, and kicks.

Very characteristic of Okinawan karate is *nekoashi-dachi*, the cat stance (figs. 11–12). Do you know why *nekoashi-dachi* is so famous? Because you use gravity to free fall by controlling your ICG with one leg. You accomplish this with your front foot in *chusoku* position, on the ball of the foot. By subtly shifting the heel up or down, you drop your knee and move your ICG forward (figs. 13–15). It is amazing that so slight a movement of the foot creates free fall (figs. 16–18). You are able to produce and transfer the energy anytime and anywhere with only this subtle heel movement. You can now move forward into your opponent's blind spot with a diagonal *hanmi* position and deliver Shuri-te's one-shot whipping punch (figs. 19–20).

If you are able to drop a knee at any time while in any stance, you can maneuver without ever becoming stuck in any one spot. If you do not understand this dropping-knee technique, you will find no meaning to the moves practiced in katas. You will simply be mimicking a kata's choreography, as if copying a new dance step. You must practice enough that this becomes a natural part of you, so you automatically drop a tiny bit for short-range action and more to reach a long-range target. If you use this method of maneuvering from the beginning to the end of a fight, you can move your ICG around anywhere outside of your body. You can deliver any technique while you are moving and at the same time, because you are moving, give your opponent no target. Therefore, you walk in martial arts, and walking is only continuous standing.

Why do modern karateka get stuck in one spot? One of the reasons is the word itself—*tachi* or *dachi* (stance). When karate moved to Japan, there was a need somehow to explain the moves. So they practiced as if in a slow-motion

Figs. 13–15 By subtly shifting the heel up and down, you drop your knee and move your ICG forward.

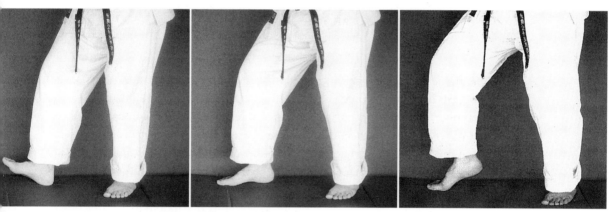

Figs. 16–18 This movement of the foot creates the fall.

Figs. 19–20 Move forward into your opponent's blind spot with a diagonal *hanmi* position.

Figs. 21–23 In Shorin-ryu, when practicing Shuri-te, the back foot is brought forward in a straight line toward its new position in front.

film, frame by frame. When they used one frozen frame to demonstrate a stance, that *tachi* became a rooted, or stuck, position. The word *tachi* belied the real meaning. There was no particular stance in early karate. This does not mean that the old karate masters did not care about stance. The truth is completely the opposite. They understood that it is meaningless to fix a stance position, because it is only important for the split second of transition that connects one part of a maneuver to another.

A few schools of Shuri-te–style karate do not bring one foot in toward the other when moving forward. Instead, the back foot is brought forward in a straight line toward its new position in front, just as we do when walking (figs. 21–23). The stance that I have discussed in this chapter is the expert level of walking. You must understand and master this way of walking, then you can perform katas with this walking technique. Old Okinawan karate masters said, "Learn from part of the final movement of the kata at the beginning." I will explain this later.

Aikido is the martial art today that understands this walking. Those people who saw Morihei Ueshiba fight were amazed and said, "He walks and delivers techniques." Now you understand this mystery. I am sure Ueshiba said (and now you can say) that you can deliver techniques because you are walking (figs. 24–25).

A contemporary karate master who also understood this walking is Mas (Masutatsu) Oyama, the founder of Kyokushin Karate. You may have heard of a little performance he did for apprentices. He made them sit on a chair, then he pressed his finger to their foreheads. When he asked them to stand up, they could not. He was not showing off his strength. He knew that without putting the ICG outside of the body, in this case at the front, they could not rise from the chair. He learned this concept when he was studying Daito-ryu Aiki Jujitsu. Unfortunately, when he passed away, this concept was not passed on to Kyokushin Kai practitioners.

Fig. 24 Morihei Ueshiba (1883–1969 A.D.), the founder of Aikido.

Fig. 25 Sokaku Takeda (1860–1943 A.D.), the father of modern Daito-ryu Aiki Jujitsu.

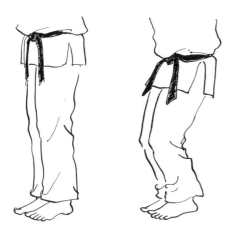

Diags. 1–2 By relaxing the muscles that support the knee joint, you consciously allow gravity to take over its pull on your body.

DROPPING-KNEE TECHNIQUE

Let me explain this dropping-knee technique in detail. By relaxing the muscles that support the knee joint, you consciously allow gravity to take over its pull on your body (diags. 1–2). From an opponent's point of view, the beginning of this dropping-knee motion is invisible because gravity controls the initial movement of the action. Since it is obvious that gravity exists everywhere and all the time, it is possible for you to move from any body position without first generating energy with a setting move, or by pushing against the ground. Because of this dropping-knee technique, you can put your ICG right in front of your opponent and produce a punch that literally goes through a target.

A person who understands this interaction between two objects in the natural world will proceed to study physics. A person who understands this in a religious way will search for a relationship between God and man. A martial artist must strive to understand the dynamic balance between one man and another. The virtue of martial arts can create harmony in all aspects of society. Even without this virtue, a society will still grow and you can learn martial art techniques. But if you recognize Divine Providence from the viewpoint of martial arts training, you will be able to see the world from a completely different perspective. Even though you think you have achieved and mastered the universal laws and techniques, you have in reality only borrowed them from the universe or God. We literally live in a borrowed world. To be complete, martial arts must embrace Divine Providence. Martial arts study holds valuable lessons for living in harmony with nature and becoming one with all forms of life in this universe.

Morihei Ueshiba was able to evade an opponent's attack because he used the ICG to become one with the opponent anywhere, at any time. He used the ICG further to be able to maneuver, grab, and defeat the opponent. In other words, find the ICG that exists between you and your opponent as soon as possible, and move into that ICG as fast as possible without letting him see your move. It is best to use *musubi-dachi* or *heisoku-dachi* stance (heels and toes together). If you slowly move forward with straightened posture and the head held high, you can move forward without letting your opponent realize it. Gravity is equal for both sides (which means gravity is not equal on both sides, because you are manipulating it to your advantage). Your opponent will never know where you will shift your weight and where you will move next. Shurite's fighters use a method of bringing in the front leg to *musubi-dachi* or *heisoku-dachi* just before moving forward. This move can be seen in a kata called *Rohai* in Tomari-te, or Kushanku (Kusanku) in Shuri-te. In Okinawan weapons katas, you commence from a forward-leaning stance. Of course, this must be thoroughly ingrained to perform quickly in a real fight, and you must never allow your energy to become deadlocked, even in a cat stance. In traditional Okinawan karate, your heels must never bear the brunt of your weight. They must always feel as if they are lifted slightly, no matter what your stance.

You will recall that early efforts to teach Okinawan karate in Japan resulted in misunderstanding. You will also recall the effects of the Industrial Revolution on karate's development. Advancements in anatomy and physiology developed as a logical extension of interest in mechanical engineering and electrical engineering, among other things. While we can understand the attempts to apply these influences to martial arts, the results produce more friction and extraneous movement than desired. Realistically, you cannot fight with this method. That is the reason we at Muso-Kai are striving to understand universal law and revive the old techniques. We practice only two things as the foundation of this technique: one, create energy by using your body as a whip; and two, produce energy ($F = MA$) through gravitational pull by dropping the knee. Many true Japanese martial arts use ICG and dropping the knee. We have discussed moving straight toward an opponent or moving in at a 45-degree angle, using *irimi* (turning an opponent's force against him by a yielding motion). But this is not everything. It is the beauty of it, yet it is also scary. In traditional Okinawan karate, you can deliver techniques at a 90-degree angle sideways without moving your body up or down. I will explain this in detail in the next chapter.

SHUKUCHI-HOU: SUDDEN ARRIVAL METHOD

How can you quickly reach an opponent who stands far away from you without running? The answer is *walk fast*. This is not a joke. In Okinawan karate, there is a foot maneuver of walking fast without letting the opponent know your intention. Here is an example. First, face your opponent (fig. 1). At the moment that you drop your knee, bring up your back leg as high as possible to your chest and use the free fall move by leaning forward (fig. 2). Do not move your upper body, including the head. Move forward with your shoulders leaning to the front and imagine your back leg stepping over a big object (figs. 3–4). This is a completely different body movement from generating energy by kicking against the ground.

Because this is, in essence, a walking move, you do not open up your body to move forward. You can move dramatically closer to your opponent while creating and increasing energy. Your body should not go up and down, especially your head, when you move forward. From the opponent's point of view, you are moving into him two-dimensionally. He sees an illusion. He sees that you are not moving, yet somehow you are suddenly closer to him. This answers the third condition of your contest with the cheetah, in that you avoid being seen by your opponent because you are moving while you seem to be not moving.

Fig. 1 Face your opponent.

Fig. 2 At the moment that you drop your knee, bring up your back leg high.

This is the secret called *shukuchi-hou*. *Shuku* means shrink, *chi* means ground, and *hou* means method. This is the only foot maneuver in the martial arts whose name translates literally into its description. We live in a three-dimensional world and are used to observing the world this way. From your opponent's point of view, using *shukuchi*, you move for a moment in a one- or two-dimensional world. In Okinawan karate, this method is used a lot. One example is to change a two-dimensional fight to a three-dimensional one by using *shukuchi* to suddenly float in the air. There are many techniques to distract the opponent and change his dimensional perspective by creating a time lag, or delayed strike. Fifteen years ago, I could use *shukuchi* for a distance of over sixteen feet. Now I can only reach about two-thirds of that length, but still I can reach an opponent long before he reacts. It is like running one hundred yards in twenty seconds without letting the opponent know your move, rather than running one hundred yards in ten seconds and telegraphing your move to him from the beginning. This is the speed and power of martial arts. The practice of martial arts is to reduce this twenty seconds to ten seconds. You are using the absolute law of relativity according to your opponent's position. To repeat what I promised earlier, there is a method to do this *shukuchi* directly sideways.

TECHNIQUE WITH NO RHYTHM

Because Okinawan karate's kicks and punches use the universal law to create energy, they are completely different in concept and technique from modern karate's kicks and punches. The ancient Japanese masters called this the "no-rhythm technique." This idea is inherent in the final level of traditional Japanese sword fighting: "You only bring up the sword and drop the sword, nothing

Figs. 3–4 Move forward with your shoulders leaning to the front and imagine your back leg stepping over a big object.

more." From a technical point of view, you use gravity as much as possible, adding the acceleration that you create with dropping the knee. This no-rhythm technique is an essential element of basic Okinawan karate. If you understand this dropping-knee theory and technique, you can punch or kick with maximum energy in any direction, even while standing on one leg.

The katas of traditional Okinawan karate begin and end with simple moves such as leaning forward a little, putting the arm forward, or standing with one leg and punching sideways. There are no dynamic or fancy kicks or punches. When I was young, I believed that these moves would not work without waist rotation and power-packed punches. But since I recognized the existence of ICG, my karate has changed.

At Muso-Kai Karate-do, higher level students practice full-contact fighting with each other, regardless of height and weight. When I practice with two-hundred-pound students, I can deliver my punch halfway (with their agreement, of course). I would never use my full punch during practice. It is dangerous to use my punch on students lighter than two hundred pounds. Once you master this kind of control and can deliver a technique from any position and appropriate to any opponent, your punch or kick will go through the body like stabbing. You just extend your punch or kick a little more forward as the old masters did. That is all.

NO REVERSE PUNCH

Until now, I have only talked about a punch delivered from the same side as your front leg. Now I will explain about a punch with the opposite arm, which you probably know as the "reverse punch." When I learned karate in Okinawa as a youngster, my master told me that there was no reverse punch in Okinawan karate. "You're kidding me!" I said in my mind, because there were many reverse punches among the katas. Karate books from both recent times and from the time when I was a youngster show pictures of reverse punches, delivering a fist with big rotation of the waist from a wide stance. When I was young, this dynamic combination was to me the true punch of karate.

In the ultimate "body culture" of the martial arts, people explained only 50 percent of the lesson by words or movements. The other 50 percent you had to master on your own. Otherwise, you would have learned only to copy and would never truly master the martial arts. Old masters learned from their masters in the same way. And of course, no one told anyone about the reason for this 50/50 mastery. Once you fully understand the meaning of dropping the knee, you will have achieved this 50 percent of learning from a master and 50 percent of learning from your own practice. Whether doing a lunge punch with the same arm as the front leg, or a reverse punch with the same arm as the back leg, the technique is the same. For a lunge punch, you drop your knee, put ICG to the front, and let gravity take over your body's fall into the punch. You do the same thing for a reverse punch, without stepping forward with your back leg. You simply drop your knee to punch.

In a lunge punch, you deliver a punch as you walk by dropping the knee. In a reverse punch, you would be too close to the opponent if you brought your back leg forward to punch. Therefore, you cannot step forward. Instead, drop your front knee slightly and place your ICG forward to punch just as you did in a lunge punch, but with the opposite arm. The back foot may slide forward a bit as you deliver the punch. This is the reason my master said "no reverse punch." Of course, you do not rotate your waist. Bring your waist forward as you do naturally when walking. It is wrong to rotate the waist to punch. It would not be as efficient if you moved your fist from point A to point B by rotating the waist. You must extend the waist by sliding forward. (Remember *gamaku?*) You can see this in katas when you perform a reverse punch. Your back leg will slide forward. Your body naturally tries to place its ICG where you want to move by sliding without using your waist.

Waist rotation wastes energy, therefore your punch is not effective. If you study karateka who have executed knockouts with reverse punches, you will see they use this sliding waist unconsciously. The true karate punch is close to a professional boxer's in this use of the waist. So why is there a rotating waist method? When karate became a sport instead of a martial art, it had to be safe for competition. Rules stated that you had to stop the punch before hitting the opponent. The way to show the judges that the punch would actually be effective was to rotate the waist in order to show how much power you could generate from one position.

Karate methods are completely different from golf or baseball, whose goal is to hit a ball as far as possible. Karate was born and developed in life or death situations. Waist rotation will not work in such a reality. You will die making a circle with a circle.

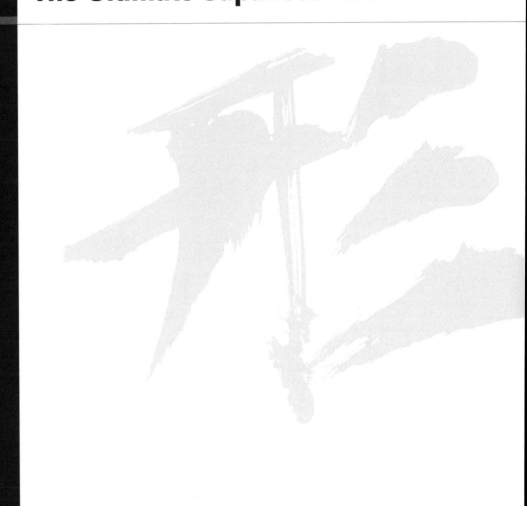

KATA

Chapter 4 **The Ultimate Japanese Art**

Thirty years ago in Okinawa, when I studied karate from the masters, I would hear "Master Itosu always walked with Naifanchi stance." This Naifanchi kata appears at first glance to be very simple. With slightly bent knees and feet about shoulder-width apart, you deliver techniques moving from side to side the way a crab walks. Hearing this, you might think "What a weird guy! A master who walked around like a crab all day?" Actually, until a hundred years ago, when Itosu created the Pinan katas for school education, most karateka began and ended their training with the study of Naifanchi.

Another story was told that Choki Motobu (see page 4), a powerful fighter nicknamed "Monkey," knew only Naifanchi kata. Of course, this was an exaggeration, but it helps illustrate my point. What is so special about this Naifanchi kata? To understand its importance, it is necessary to understand the classification of Okinawan karate kata, which can be organized into three main categories:

1. Basic (or Ultimate)
2. Practice
3. Application

A basic kata retains the very essence of karate while striving to achieve the ultimate form based on this essence. A practice kata repeats the same techniques many times within the kata. These katas are seen often in modern dojos and are an effective drill for improving student proficiency. An application kata trains a student to deliver real-fight techniques. It is a collection of offensive and defensive moves to be used against one or more opponents. These katas' creators based them on real fights, thinking about foot maneuvers, body control and hand technique combinations. The disadvantage is that they were based on their creator's favorite techniques, so they will not necessarily work for everyone. A person who is not able to jump very well would waste his time trying to learn fighting skills from an application kata employing lots of jumps and kicks. He would learn more from sparring drills in his dojo than from practicing those katas.

NAIFANCHI KATA

The most important and necessary element of martial arts study is found in the basic katas because they have retained the concept and essence of controlled body movement. Naifanchi I (*Sho-dan*), II (*Ni-dan*), and III (*San-dan*) have condensed this essence of Okinawan karate into simple, crablike moves.

While there was originally only one Naifanchi, today it is taught as three katas. The most important is the first one. The other two are application katas. The idea and technique of Naifanchi have not been passed on completely to either modern Japanese or Okinawan karate. This loss is critical. Naifanchi is the basic kata. Though deceptively simple, it is the most difficult kata, because it holds all the essence of karate and no one can compromise its execution. While learning Naifanchi, keep in mind that it is the zenith of the martial arts. Its meaning has been passed on only by oral tradition. It took thirty years for me to understand completely its technical concept. I believe there are fewer than ten karate practitioners who completely understand Naifanchi and perform it. The purpose of this book is to help you toward a complete understanding of and ability to perform Naifanchi.

INSIGHT INTO NAIFANCHI

Explication of Naifanchi: I

To make it easier to understand Naifanchi, let's focus on foot and body maneuvers. To begin, stand with feet together and relax (fig. 1). This is called *musubi-dachi* or *heisoku-dachi*, the informal attention stance. The name is not important. What is important is to stand with the feet as close together as possible. Next, look directly to the right side and slowly cross the left foot over to the right side of the right foot (fig. 2). This foot maneuver is called *kakeashi-dachi*, the crossing

Fig. 1 Stand with feet together and relax.

Fig. 2 Look directly to the right side and slowly cross the left foot over to the right side of the right foot.

Figs. 3–4 Once both feet are aligned, lift the right foot from the ground without moving the head up or down.

stance. Once both feet are aligned (fig. 3), lift the right foot from the ground without moving the head up or down (fig. 4). The right foot will make a half circle as you bend your knee and bring your foot up high in front of your body. Then place this foot down to your right in Naifanchi stance (fig. 5). When bringing up and placing the right foot, never lose your posture or the head's balance either up and down or sideways. At the beginning, it is difficult to perform without any extraneous movement. The essential principle of Oki-

nawan karate is to move without seeming to do so. Many people have learned this kata without having learned the essence of Naifanchi, as explained in the rest of this chapter. This vital point has been lost. The right hand now extends directly sideways. Some karate styles call this movement *nami gaeshi* (returning wave), but the name has no bearing on understanding the essence. Next, the left elbow strikes toward the right side as your right hand moves in to become the elbow's target. Follow with a left downward block and a right punch toward the left side.

As explained in Chapters 2 and 3, set your ICG to create energy while walking, then use it in this sideways crab-walk. Walk sideways just

Diag. 1 Your ICG is already in the place you will stand in Naifanchi-*dachi*.

Fig. 5 Place the foot down to your right in Naifanchi stance.

Figs. 6–7 You are walking forward.

Figs. 8–9 Master level of Naifanchi. Walk sideways just as if you were walking forward.

Figs. 10–11 The head stays put and only the body bends to the right side.

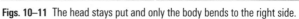

as if you were walking forward (figs. 8–9). This is the master level of Naifanchi.

As shown in figure 2 and diagram 1, your ICG is already in the place you will stand in Naifanchi-*dachi*. Imagine yourself standing on only the left leg, then drop the right knee. At the beginning or middle level of study, the body must act like a supple willow branch, so that the head stays put and only the body bends to the right side (figs. 10–11).

Figs. 1–4 Extend the right arm sideways, and bring in the right arm to meet the left elbow strike. Then execute a whipping left downward block and a right whipping punch to the left.

Explication of Naifanchi: II

Remember that Okinawan karate uses a walking technique, leaning toward the ICG, to create energy. This differs from today's karate, which relies on the concept of action-reaction movement, with a rigid or deadlocked body. Conditions which create energy (such as leaning toward the ICG) are *jitsu*, while conditions which do not create energy (such as a rigid, upright body) are *kyo*. *Jitsu* designates the existence of something; *kyo* implies its absence. *Jitsu* is real; *kyo* is empty. Standing on both legs is *kyo*, because your energy has become deadlocked and cannot be used at this moment. Standing on one leg is *jitsu*, because you are using your ICG to create an energy-filled space. In these pictures, extending the right arm sideways is the indication of ICG. Bring in the right arm to meet the left elbow strike. Try not to move any other body parts much. Then execute a whipping left downward block and a right whipping punch to the left (figs. 1–4).

Next, look to the left. Cross the right foot over the left, aligning it parallel to the left foot. Lift the left foot high in front of your body, with left knee bent to the side, then drop it to the left in Naifanchi-*dachi*. This much is a mirror image of what we did in Explication I. Even when the feet are closely aligned, the ICG must be at the side. *Kyo* is where the body actually is and *jitsu* is at the side. When a man walks, his body naturally tilts a little to the front. Apply this feeling to Naifanchi and use your ICG to create energy by turning your head to the side. At the same time that you place the left foot on the ground, execute a right inward block to the front, followed by a left inward block and a right downward block to the front, then a left back-knuckle strike to the front, with the

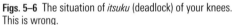

Figs. 5–6 The situation of *itsuku* (deadlock) of your knees. This is wrong.

Figs. 7–8 You can avoid this *itsuku* by executing a right outward block to the front.

right fist just beneath the left elbow. Be sure to apply Shuri-te's whipping motion without much movement of the body.

The old masters said "*Metsuke* (eye contact with the imaginary target—in this case, facing to the side) is the most important technique in Naifanchi." If your eyes are focused on your intended target area, your ICG will move more easily to that point. Beginners tend to shift their weight to the supporting leg before moving, because their bodies cannot hold them yet without shifting balance. Shifting your weight deadlocks the body's energy as you lift the other leg (figs. 5–6). You can avoid this *itsuku* (deadlock) by executing a right outward block to the front (figs. 7–8). This use of the opposite leg muscles eliminates any obvious movement of the body and disguises any shifting of weight. Up to this point, it is still easy to move muscles in the opposite direction from the body's actual movement.

Explication of Naifanchi: III

The uniqueness of Naifanchi is that you can stand on two legs with *jitsu* (reality) or stand on one leg with *kyo* (emptiness), or vice versa. This ability to generate energy regardless of your position makes possible the 90-degree sideways move that Okinawan karate proudly contributes to the world. It is possible to move sideways only if you can move your muscles independently of one another. You must be able to control each muscle individually.

You are now ready for Naifanchi's next move. Without losing your balance or posture, bring the left foot up in front of your body with the left knee pointing

Fig. 1 Without losing your balance or posture, bring the left foot up in front of your body.

Fig. 2 You are standing on two legs with *kyo. Jitsu* is in the invisible third leg supporting your ICG.

toward your left. Do not move the supporting leg at all (fig. 1). Your natural tendency will be to shift your weight to the supporting leg, thereby extending it somewhat from your original knees-slightly-bent position. This extending reaction makes the body stick and deadlocks your energy because it shifts the ICG to the actual center of gravity inside the body.

While lifting the leg, bring your left arm across in front of your body, left elbow still lightly resting on the right fist (fig. 8 on the previous page). This counterbalances the leg movement and makes it easier to control your balance. By using an opposite muscle, your body will not feel as much need to shift weight to the right. From here, the left arm strikes to the left side as the left foot is placed into Naifanchi stance. Next, lift your right leg in the same manner as you just lifted the left, replacing it in Naifanchi stance. Bring the left arm (still resting on the right fist) in a block across the front of your body, then execute a double punch to your left side.

From another person's point of view, your body will bend at an angle. At this split second, you are standing on two legs with *kyo. Jitsu* is in the invisible third leg supporting your ICG (fig. 2). Keep this in mind as you practice the moves above.

Once you have mastered this technique, you will always be able to create this "third leg." Standing on two legs can at times feel like standing on three legs, and at other times it can feel like standing on one leg. Standing on one leg

Figs. 3–7 All tsuki must be executed according to Shuri-te's whipping technique.

will feel like being balanced on two legs. This seems to make no sense, until you have mastered Naifanchi. Then it makes perfect sense. This is the mysterious and marvelous concept of *kyo* and *jitsu* of martial arts. To master the split-second changes in motion is the hardest thing about this *kyo-jitsu*.

To finish Naifanchi kata, repeat these same moves to the opposite side. All tsuki, blocks, and strikes must be executed according to Shuri-te's whipping technique (figs. 3–7) Remember, though, that the main concept of Naifanchi kata is in the foot and body maneuvers. Hand techniques are just the supporting moves to facilitate this foot movement.

Fig. 1 Put your ICG in a pocket of space just outside the body.

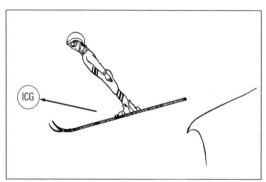

Diag. 1 A ski jumper puts his ICG in front of his body in order to fly farther.

Explication of Naifanchi: IV

Even if one can move sideways, it is hard to bring the leg up high while sliding to the side. The old masters said "Don't move your head! The most important thing is *metsuki*! Open up the chest and put the hip out a little!" The first two are clear now, but how about the last one? Why open up the chest and stick out the hip? The answer is that making this posture creates a pocket of space just outside the body (fig. 1). Put your ICG in this space. This way the body floats even though your feet are on the ground.

It is the same as a ski jumper who puts his Imaginary Center of Gravity in front of his body in order to fly farther. Diagram 1 shows the powerful vector created by the ski jumper. The Kushanku kata and the Rohai kata use this same principle.

Diags. 2–4 As you begin to lift your leg, this invisible force automatically pulls your foot up high.

Imagine a large rubber band attached between this pocket of space and your leg, creating tension as you stand. As you begin to lift your leg, this invisible force automatically pulls your foot up high (diags. 2–4). In this way, you are able to maintain your posture. You apply this concept subconsciously in everyday walking. As gravity takes over, the body falls forward without contracting any muscles that would cause an action-reaction momentum. This enables you to control the distance of each step and even to hold the leg up in the air for a few moments. By controlling distance and rhythm, you have an advantage over your opponent. Manipulation of *kyo* and *jitsu* is the most important foot maneuver you can learn. The purpose of Naifanchi is to change the direction of this technique from the front to the side.

At the final level of mastery, you will be able to walk to the side as easily as you now walk to the front. Because you can contract each muscle independently of another, you can move to the right while putting your weight with *kyo* to your left and vice versa. Therefore, it is possible to simultaneously employ defensive and offensive techniques. Naifanchi contains this superior concept of the martial arts. Though some of the essence of Naifanchi has been lost over the generations, we are fortunate that at least the skeleton has been passed on orally among the Okinawan people.

Explication of Naifanchi: V

It is possible to use the *shukuchi* (shrinking ground) technique directly to the side if one masters this next level. You must work to control the moving leg by

Fig. 1 You must work to control the moving leg by adjusting the knee drop of the supporting leg.

Fig. 2 You control the width of the stance.

Fig. 3 Morihei Ueshiba stood with his toes pointed at a 45-degree angle outward so he could move quickly.

Fig. 4 Practicing this Naifanchi technique from *musubi-dachi*, it is easier to master.

Diag. 1 Naifanchi looks like a chair standing normally, even though the legs on one side are missing.

Diag. 2 A physically coordinated person can stand on one leg and balance herself.

Diag. 3 A flexible person can even bring one leg over the head while balancing perfectly on the other leg.

adjusting the knee drop of the supporting leg (figs. 1–2). This is the dream of the *shukuchi* technique. Even Ueshiba, who recognized the ICG, stood with his toes pointed at a 45-degree angle outward so he could move quickly (fig. 3). If one can move sideways (the hardest direction for man to move without changing the direction of the toe), he can move to any point of a 360-degree circle by only shifting his ICG.

It is easier to master the Naifanchi technique while practicing it from *musubi-dachi* or *heisoku-dachi* (fig. 4). If one attempted from the beginning to learn the maneuver while using a wider stance, then even exceptionally talented and patient people would give up their practice.

A few masters had been told in their younger days to practice Naifanchi in a rice field. They complained that it was very difficult because of the mud. However, their masters were showing mercy because the mud actually helped stabilize the body and facilitate balance. It was as if there were a third leg holding the body, while you stood on one leg and lifted the second. The ultimate Naifanchi uses this "third leg" to hold the body suspended in motion, or to shift body weight without moving other muscles.

At a Muso-Kai dojo, one of the higher black belt students commented after seeing the author's Naifanchi, "It looks like a chair standing normally, even though the legs on one side are missing" (diag. 1). No one can see the chair standing only on the legs of one side without visualizing the imaginary legs. No one can understand the true meaning we are pursuing without recognizing this idea.

Here is an example of the difference between *itsuku* and non-*itsuku*. Any modern Chinese Kung-fu practitioner who is physically coordinated can stand on one leg and balance herself (diag. 2). Those who are very flexible can even bring one leg over the head while balancing perfectly on the other leg (diag. 3). However, this is not martial arts, but gymnastics. It is impossible to stand with an imaginary leg without understanding this essence of martial arts. This can only be achieved by people who have learned to move different muscles in different directions at the same time.

KAN-NO-ME: THE OBSERVING EYE

Kan-no-me is the inner eye (sense) that is able to "see" the imaginary leg without regular eyes. Without comprehension of *kan-no-me*, no one can understand Okinawan karate's kata. If you can master placing the ICG to the side without bouncing the body, you can certainly move very easily to the front and back. No other martial art practices this sideways, completely smooth foot maneuver that retains balance while in motion. It is proof of the excellence (and difficulty) of this move that both novices and experts practice this maneuver in Okinawa. You can now understand why the masters said "Begin with Naifanchi and end with Naifanchi."

Naifanchi *Ni-dan* (II) and *San-dan* (III) are only variations of the techniques learned in Naifanchi *Sho-dan* (I). Once you master the first Naifanchi, the second and third will seem much easier. It was an old belief that you should teach the hardest technique first in martial arts, also that you should master only one thing at a time before moving on to the next. Naifanchi is a typical example of this idea. A person who can employ the dropping-knee technique to maneuver without moving the body up and down can perform any kata in Shuri-te. He will also understand the true meaning of the kata and be able to apply it to any situation. Without this comprehension, all practice is meaningless. Even a talented martial artist needs about a year of hard training to master Naifanchi. But if a master demanded this kind of training and dedication today, his dojo would be empty of students in three weeks.

In Muso-Kai, students begin their study with katas that appeal to an audience and basics that develop physical strength. Even after attaining the levels of *San-dan* (third-degree black belt) or *Yon-dan* (fourth-degree black belt), they begin Naifanchi study with tears of frustration. Because of our modern, comfortable civilization, people no longer have the opportunities to build up their bodies from daily life as they did in older times. Therefore, students must first learn how to use *gamaku*, as we discussed in Chapter 1. At Muso-Kai, color belts look at the katas of black belts and are eager to learn the most appealing ones. But when they look at the kata of higher black belts, it is a different story. The higher black belts learn the real traditional kata. Those color belts see their models just standing and struggling to move sideways, and think they do not want to learn this Naifanchi.

One day, a *Yon-dan* black belt who had been struggling with Naifanchi for a year suddenly stopped, awestricken because he finally understood its true meaning. He just stood rooted to the spot and could not move. He was almost in tears. He had always placed high in U.S. tournaments, but had never truly understood the essence of what he was doing. All his master could do was to say to him, "What is past is of no consequence. It is enough that you now understand and respect the true meaning and challenge of Naifanchi." As you travel upward

Figs. 1–2 Master Shoshin Nagamine (1907–1997 A.D.), practicing Naifanchi.

on the path of the martial arts, you realize that after a certain point, you can only be self-taught. You must use all your prior knowledge and experience to search out the answers for yourself. This *Yon-dan* black belt had finally achieved enlightenment.

Do not forget that there is more to Naifanchi as the highest expression of the true martial arts. After you are able to move sideways, you must execute techniques with Shuri-te's whipping motion. And, of course, tsuki must be executed with equal facility to the side or the front. Your tsuki must have power (not just physical strength) to knock down an opponent. You will strive toward the master level when you can deliver your tsuki without the willowlike body movement and without whipping.

At the master level, these will be done inside the body. If someone watches a master executing tsuki, it will look as if he is just putting his arm out to the target, but the target will certainly feel that this is more than the simple extension of an arm. A student with martial arts talent will take at least three years to master these techniques. In Shuri-te–style karate, demonstrating Naifanchi kata is the true test of a student's ability.

The author has studied all possible publications and videos related to martial arts, in both Japanese and English. Among these is a book by Shoshin Nagamine, the founder of Shorin-ryu ("pine forest"). His demonstrations of lifting up the leg in Naifanchi *Sho-dan* are splendid. In our time, no other pictures have ever shown such a splendid rendition of Naifanchi (figs. 1–2). It shows not only his martial art talent but also his dedication to practice.

Choki Motobu surpassed even Nagamine. His Naifanchi shows the final level of kata, enabling him to fight, yet still retain the essence of martial arts. He demonstrated that there is no need to rely on physical strength or muscle

Figs. 3–4 Master Choki Motobu (1870–1944 A.D.), practicing Naifanchi.

development in Naifanchi or any other kata (figs. 3–4). He used just a little internal muscle contraction, never action-reaction. He performed Naifanchi without showing how he had created energy, using gravity and invisible leg (*kyo-jitsu*) balance. This is the perfect martial arts concept.

Someone looking at figures 3–4 might think that they were taken by a camera with a high-speed shutter. No such camera existed at that time. If he performed Naifanchi slowly enough for the camera to capture this moment, it was a superhuman feat.

There is a legend of Motobu's return to Okinawa as an old man. Choshin Chibana (figs. 5–7), who was the founder of Shorin ("small forest," different from the above Shorin-ryu) and a pupil of Anko Itosu, asked Motobu to perform his Naifanchi in front of Chibana's students. Those students said Motobu's kata was boring and scoffed at this old man who could not quite show physical strength and could not keep his balance. On the other hand, Chibana was mad with joy and just exclaimed "This is it! This is it!" He meant that he had just witnessed "the" martial art. This episode shows that Chibana had *kan-no-me*, observing eyes, and how few people had observing eyes, even in those days.

Another legend of Motobu's Naifanchi involves Shoshin Nagamine. At Nagamine's dojo, there was a picture of Motobu performing Naifanchi. One day, because Nagamine was writing a book, it became necessary to take pictures of his katas. He asked a well-known Okinawan cameraman to do the photography. When the photographer entered the dojo, he was mesmerized by Motobu's picture. Nagamine noticed him staring at the picture and said, "That is my master, the famous Choki 'Monkey' Motobu." [He was as nimble as a monkey.] The photographer came out of his trance and said, "Oh! This picture

Figs. 5–6 Choshin Chibana (1885–1969 A.D.), the founder of Shorin, practicing Passai.

Fig. 7 Choshin Chibana.

is alive!" He did not mean it was moving. He meant that there was life in it. Seeing the picture is understanding. Understanding is seeing with insight.

Motobu performed the perfect Naifanchi. The photographer who snapped Motobu's image was able to capture a moment of martial art essence. The photographer who saw the picture was able to see the essence captured in that frame. And Nagamine kept the legend of it. I am fortunate to have lived at a time when karate was still part of daily life.

SHIKO-DACHI

There are a lot of strategic differences between Shuri-te and Naha-te. Shuri-te's Naifanchi stance places the feet about shoulder-width apart with knees bent as if sitting on a chair to control the ICG. On the other hand, the present-day stance of Naha-te is much wider and deeper, about twice as wide as Shuri-te. The thighs are parallel to the ground and the knees bent at a 90-degree angle. In this position, it is hard to move around. However, you will notice that the person in figure 1 is not deadlocked. This is *shiko-dachi*, the Sumo stance. In Shuri-te's Naifanchi, it is possible to make a pocket of space, but it is not possible

Fig. 1 *Shiko-dachi*. Even though the stance of the practitioner is wide and deep, he is not deadlocked.

Fig. 2 For the sensation of floating, the word "jump" is used at the beginning.

Figs. 3–4 You will be able to bring your legs up high without moving other parts of the body.

to do the same thing in Naha-te's. Picture an imaginary V with the tops at either side of the pelvis and the bottom sticking into the ground (diag. 1). Because of this support, both legs can lift up. In other words, it is like a horse on a merry-go-round. There is a pole supporting the horse, so its legs can be in the air. This is called dividing the pelvis.

There is a breathing technique to lower the *tanden* (the source of energy within the abdomen) and stick out the pelvis to create an imaginary leg to stand on. Even though you are in a wide stance, you can lower the pelvis and lift your leg. The difference between Shuri-te and Naha-te is in this point. Therefore, it is hard to learn them both until a student has reached a high level. They look the same to beginners and middle-level practitioners, but are different in essence. Muso-Kai students who learned performance katas at the color belt level start learning

Figs. 5–6 You could also deliver a kick from a wide stance with no shift of weight.

Diag. 1

Fig. 7 Many practitioners are deadlocked in kata tournaments.

traditional katas after they reach black belt. During practice, they are asked to jump from any position or stance without additional movement. It is hard to imagine the sensation of floating, so we use the word "jump" at the beginning (fig. 2).

Figures 3–4 show that after mastering this level you will be able to bring your legs up high without moving other parts of the body, even from a wide stance. Using the same concept, you could also deliver a kick from a wide stance with no shift of weight to warn your opponent of the impending strike (figs. 5–6). As long as one can "float" the body, he can kick in any direction. In a present-day Naha-te kata tournament, a competitor moves from point A to point B with a sliding maneuver. At point B, he stands wide and deep, putting himself in a deadlocked position, then executes the next technique. Without *kan-no-me* and imaginary legs, these katas have no energy; they are deadlocked (fig. 7).

Fig. 1 Sumo champion Kitanoumi (1953 A.D.–), performing *shiko-dachi*.

Diag. 1 An illustration of Iizasa Iga-no-kami Ienao, Japanese sword master.

Diag. 2 The bamboo leaves and branches he sat on did not bend or break.

FLOATING

There is a famous anecdote about this "floating" in the Japanese Kendo world. It refers to Iizasa Iga-no-kami Ienao (C. 1386–?), who was the founder of Tenshin Shoden Katori Shinto-ryu, one of the main schools of Japanese swordsmanship (diag. 1). Many practitioners of swordsmanship visited Ienao while he lived at Katori. Some of the more heedless challenged him as a way of becoming famous. He brought the challengers to his garden, which was covered with bamboo bushes (small broadleaf bushes which grow to a height of no more than two feet). Placing a cushion on one of these bushes, he sat and faced them. The bamboo leaves and branches he sat on did not bend or break (diag. 2). He was "floating." Of course, even those naive challengers had *kan-no-me* enough to see Ienao's real strength. Then they feared him and left his house without fighting. Whether or not this story is true, it tells us that Japanese swordsmen recognized and understood floating.

Fig. 2 Gichin Funakoshi (1868–1957 A.D.), the founder of Shotokan.

Fig. 3 Jigoro Kano (1860–1938 A.D.), the founder of Judo.

In Japan today, Sumo practitioners are among the few who are aware of this technique. The talented champion Kitanoumi (fig. 1) recognized and executed this float, even when his ranking in Sumo was low. When he was still new in Sumo competition, those who were champions observed, "That young guy, Kitanoumi, can bring up his leg from *shiko-dachi* (deep, bent-knee stance)." He was floating, of course. It was inevitable that Sumo would become Japan's national sport. The Sumo wrestlers recognized, understood, and executed this floating as the most important technique for fighting in a small, round ring.

In 1922, Okinawan karate was introduced at a public performance at Judo's mecca, the Kodokan. Gichin Funakoshi (fig. 2) showed Kushanku kata, and Shinkin Gima, who was the pupil of Anko Itosu, demonstrated Naifanchi. Among the assembly were Judo practitioners who had *kan-no-me* to see the floating. Jigoro Kano (fig. 3), founder of Judo, and his top students asked many questions of Funakoshi and Gima. They were amazed to see that Okinawan karate had a stance like Judo's *jigotai* (wide, open-leg stance) and that Naifanchi executed floating techniques from that position. This is another example of early martial artists who recognized the importance of and practiced a floating technique. As remarkable as this ability to float is, in the final level of Naifanchi the body must float even before starting the kata, while standing in *musubi-dachi*. Keep this in mind.

Fig. 1 Photo of Tesshu Yamaoka (1836–1888 A.D.), the founder of *Muto-ryu* ("without a sword" style).

MASTERING WITH HUNDRED-TIMES PRACTICE

Achieving finesse in body control techniques will enable you to create an illusion in your opponent's eyes. Like a magician, you will be able to hide your movements from your observers. Your goal is to place your ICG at a point that seems a safe distance from your opponent's perspective, but is actually the optimum distance for you. Because of your well-practiced finesse, you will be able to execute techniques while your opponent finds it impossible to respond. Punches, kicks, and foot and body maneuvers in Okinawan karate are based on this idea. Because it treats the human body as a weapon, it has as much depth as Japanese swordsmanship, which is considered one of the ultimate martial arts.

The pinnacle of swordsmanship expertise is winning without a sword against a sword-wielding opponent. Shinkage-ryu, an ancient school of sword fighting, was famous for this. Tesshu Yamaoka (fig. 1), who founded *Muto-ryu* ("without a sword" style), achieved this ideal. Okinawan karate has been based from the beginning on empty-hand battle against enemies with weapons. Obviously, it is outstanding in both concept and technique.

Historically, traditional Okinawan karate was passed in secret from one generation to the next. As a result, manuscript documentation is extremely rare. But even though there are no manuscripts, this culture of body-mastery is in the blood of the Okinawan people. Each one of their bodies is a manuscript for Okinawan karate. Achieving total body control by mastering this body-manuscript is the true art of Okinawan karate. Practice is the only way to fulfill this goal. This is the self-discipline of "hundred-times practice" and the philosophy of karate as being very personal to each individual. For this reason, traditional

Okinawan masters disliked putting a name to a karate style. Individual practice is your most effective route to reaching mastery.

However, Okinawan karate is not perfect. Much has been lost over the centuries. Among these are a technique for executing continuous techniques, how to read fighting distance, and *Shinpo* (heart, soul, and mind control), a technique for psychological tactics. Because of secrecy and the limited opportunity to teach others, these were not passed down. Information gleaned from a real fight was practiced in secret. This is why Muso-Kai Okinawa Karate-do promotes the study of kata, in addition to several different types of tournament fighting.

Bushi (warriors) of long ago completely understood the importance of these techniques. Thus the legend of "Itosu walks with Naifanchi-*dachi*" was told and retold. Now the reader can understand that this meant Itosu could subconsciously move in any direction with ICG, even in his everyday life. This level was achieved not only by Itosu but also by other Okinawan *bushi* who recognized and understood Itosu's feat.

After learning to float the body from Naifanchi-dachi or *shiko-dachi*, just execute strikes, kicks, or other techniques while floating. In traditional martial arts, the levels of mastering body control are as follows: hardest, foot maneuvers; moderately difficult, body maneuvers; and easiest, hand maneuvers. No matter how beautiful or dramatic a hand maneuver is, the hand technique alone does not float—its energy is deadlocked. Without the floating created by feet and/or body, the hand maneuver is ineffective. It is impossible to comprehend the meaning of martial arts without understanding the concept of deadlocked energy. Otherwise, no matter how many kata one knows and can perform, they will be only an acrobatic demonstration. However, if you understand the essence of Naifanchi, the figures in any kata can be used for meaningful practice.

CHANGE

Chapter **5** | **Kata in Martial Arts**

T oday's karate owes its existence to Anko Itosu, who was the master of Shuri-te. He realized that as society expanded and modernized, it would become increasingly more difficult to pass karate on to the next generation. He decided to incorporate the study of karate into the educational system. To accomplish this, he changed techniques to make them safer and easier to under-stand, excluding all the killing techniques that were part of the original karate. From time to time, he was criticized by other Okinawan karate masters for tam-pering with tradition, but without Itosu's foresight, knowledge of karate would not have spread.

His struggle was how to preserve and popularize karate in a society which had no more need for fighting, and how to change the traditional fight-to-the-death karate into a sport. With this new focus, karate study became very popular. But even though he successfully fulfilled his goals, his changes caused many dilemmas.

CHANGES IN KATA

First, let's discuss the analysis of kata. Analysis explains the techniques within a kata and how to use them against an opponent. Ninety-nine percent of modern-day karate masters do not know how Itosu simplified kata and therefore do not know how to analyze them. Because they lack knowledge of the historical back-ground, they end up with distorted kata.

Of particular concern is the application of two techniques—*shuto-uke* (sword hand block) and *sei-ken* (clenched fist)—which are found in most katas. These two are completely misunderstood and misused. One reason is in the terms themselves. Everyone thinks *shuto* is a technique that uses the hand like a sword or a knife, as the definition implies; therefore, the technique becomes deadlocked.

Figs. 1–8 Originally the term *shuto-uke* meant striking, blocking, grabbing, and guarding.

Figs. 9–10 In *shuto-uke*, each individual part of the arm, including the back of the hand, palm of the hand, and side of the hand, is used.

Figs. 11–12 *Sei-ken* should imply strike, hit, or stab.

Figs. 13–14 Striking with extended, rigid fingers, or *nukite*.

Fig. 1 The first level is to create energy by physical movement.

Fig. 2 The second level uses the energy between oneself and the opponent.

Fig. 3 The last level uses the energy discussed in the universal laws.

The scope of the term itself is too limited to encompass the essence of traditional karate's *shuto-uke*. Historically, this move can push the opponent; strike the opponent's upper or middle body; strike the opponent's attacking arm, or leg; block from inside or outside; grab the opponent's body, arm, or leg; hook; parry; and guard (figs. 1–8). All these possibilities are intrinsic in one technique. Modern *shuto-uke*'s usage is completely different from traditional *shuto-uke*, which employed each individual part of the arm, including the back of the hand, palm of the hand, and side of the hand, as well as the entire arm itself (figs. 9–10). It is the same story for *sei-ken*. *Sei-ken* should imply strike, hit, stab, or *nukite* (strike with one to four extended, rigid fingers) (figs. 11–14). Today's *sei-ken* is a punch which relies only on muscle strength with a big movement of the body. Since modern sports karate avoided considering the ICG, today's practitioners think that it will not work otherwise. This is completely wrong. There can be no proper analysis of kata in modern karate which does not consider the essential ideas of traditional karate.

DEADLOCKED KATA

Whether your efforts produce a good kata or a bad kata depends upon which theories are applied to generate energy and how they are applied. The first level is to create energy by physical movement (fig. 1). The second level uses the energy between oneself and the opponent (fig. 2). These are the only theories applied and used in sports karate. The last level uses the energy discussed in the universal laws (fig. 3). When we look back through human history, we find there is one more universal law: time.

Fig. 4 *Mona Lisa* by Leonardo da Vinci.

Fig. 5 *The Thinker* by Rodin.

Fig. 6 Ballet incorporates pauses in the action.

Fig. 7 Kabuki's *mie* create pause in the action. Performed by Koshiro Matsumoto as Benkei in *Kanjincho*. © Shochiku.

As you study the history of mankind, you will discover how much of man's efforts have been spent on attempting to control time and gravity. Science fiction's time machine is a manifestation of this strong desire. Paintings and sculptures are the fruit of the artist's efforts to preserve an image or idea beyond his time (figs. 4–5). A musician composes a work that he hopes will carry his ideas far beyond his years on earth. In the realm of physical culture, ballet and Kabuki (classical Japanese theater) devise pauses in the motion or action which imprint a lasting impression on the audience's memory (figs. 6–7). These are all examples of taking a moment of *do* (moving energy) and freezing it into *sei* (calm stillness). The Japanese martial arts, too, have spent much effort on controlling time, but in a different way, without an actual pause. If one simply pauses, one will be deadlocked, momentarily anchored in place, then struck by one's opponent.

In martial arts in which fights are a matter of life and death, there is a way to pause that is completely opposite from the pause of ballet or Kabuki. Because the length of time for each of two people involved in a fight is the same, one will try to execute more moves than the other so as to better control time. But if he simply speeds up his physical movement, the opponent will also increase speed to match, block, and counterattack. In the end, the time length will be the same for each fighter. It is just like the cheetah's speed. The way to increase your speed must be different, so your opponent cannot see. Foot and body maneuvers in martial arts were born from the concept that the opponent could not see and that your energy would not be deadlocked, so you could execute many moves before your opponent had time to catch up.

Your goal is, in a one-minute fight, to give your opponent his one minute while you create two minutes' worth of time for yourself. In other words, you must find a way to execute twice the number of moves as your opponent can achieve in the same amount of time. In a normal fighting competition, one must have 120 percent more strength than the opponent in order to win. This applies to time, too. Therefore, it is important to create for yourself twice the "time" length to use against the opponent. Karate as a martial art is the best physical culture for learning how to use gravity and time relatively.

Those so-called karate styles which do not contain the principles of time and gravity do not understand the essence of the martial arts. Kata should be the ultimate fusion of extreme efficiency and body control. It is a waste of time and energy to learn the kata without mastering the efficiency of the moves. This type of kata just makes the moves deadlocked. If there is time for it, one should practice basic weight training and sparring. *Bu* (combat) presupposes rational, logical calculation to achieve the most efficient results. Some martial artists love mastering the grace and beauty, without questioning the essential purpose of the kata. Their kata and *kumite* (sparring or fighting) are not side-by-side team-work. They do not realize that without mastering kata, there can be no kumite as a martial art. The concept for mastering kata is the same as for mastering kumite.

Except for Naifanchi, which is the one kata containing the pure essence of theory, most of Shuri-te's katas are only training and application katas. In Tomari-te, *Rohai* uses universal energy, as do Gojushiho (Useishi) and Kushanku in Shuri-te. Kushanku is especially good for developing the ability to float. Remember, this is different from jumping. In Naha-te, *Sanchin* is a basic (ultimate) kata and *Suparinpei* reaches the last level of energy application, applying the universal laws.

Of the more than seventy katas developed by various masters, most have been lost. There are many reasons for this loss. The main reason is that there was no need for them. Those katas created for specific persons worked only for persons of the same height, flexibility, etc., which restricted their benefit to the majority of practitioners. The katas which have survived to the present day contain the essential moves that apply to any person who practices them. These surviving katas teach continuous movement, without the energy becoming deadlocked. This is the purpose and meaning of Okinawan karate.

When *kyo* is static or still, then *jitsu* is active or moving. When *kyo* is active, *jitsu* is static. When a person completes executing a technique to finish the opponent, he must move to another position to be ready for the next move. Even if the body looks rooted in place from a third person's point of view, the Imaginary Center of Gravity and actual center of gravity must not be in the same spot. Otherwise, the karateka is deadlocked and the technique is useless. In martial arts, the concept of stillness in activity and activity in stillness applies more to body control than to the body-mind synthesis of karate philosophy. The Okinawan katas last only as long as one could perform them with one breath at full speed, thus avoiding any chance of becoming deadlocked while drawing a breath. It may seem that there are some moments where there is a pause in kata, for instance during the execution of *shuto*. These are more to invite the opponent to make the next move, than a pause per se. You should, as always, avoid becoming deadlocked here.

Kata is absolutely necessary for the final level of mastering the art. Up to now, you have been told that it is of the utmost importance to follow the katas exactly as the masters originally conceived them. You have been cautioned to never make exceptions to any technique. This next statement will sound like a complete contradiction to that. At the final level of kata study, the kata will be for you only. At this level, you would not perform your kata for anyone except your master. You would show your kata to and receive advice from this master only. In martial arts, there are three steps: *shu* (following the rules), *ha* (assimilation of the rules for your own understanding), and *li* (liberation to the next stage, where your mind and body have become the rules). Only a few karate practitioners ever reach the *ha* level. After thirty years of practice, I have finally reached the *ha* level and can see the entrance to *li*. After achieving *li*, you no longer need the kata in order to learn. You have become the kata. You completely comprehend and are in total harmony with your world.

This means all the concepts, techniques, and enlightenment have become one with the person. Life becomes karate. Karate at any moment is as natural as breathing. Therefore, there is no longer a need for kata. Kata was the means to this end. This is the level of freedom from all thought. The author, founder of Muso-Kai (meaning, "without effort or conscious thought"), established the dojo based on pursuit of this freedom.

Figs. 1–2 Taikyoku Shodan. Move your ICG out to your left.

Fig. 3 Extend your left leg out and behind to your left.

Fig. 4 Execute left *gedan-uke* with a whipping motion.

Figs. 5–7 Maneuver through *kakeashi-dachi, musubi-dachi,* and *nekoashi-dachi.*

Fig. 8 Bring the right foot into *zenkutsu-dachi,* and deliver a right whipping punch.

REBIRTH OF KATA

The study of Naifanchi kata prompts two questions: first, is it possible to use Naifanchi kata for basic practice in today's subdued martial arts? And second, if it is possible, can Naifanchi be reborn as a method for today's kata performances? The answer to both these questions is "Yes!" Any kata could be used to explain these possibilities. In this case, we'll use Taikyoku *Shodan.* In karate today, this kata is only for beginners. However, by adding all the elements that have been explained so far, this novice's kata can become a master's kata. If necessary, refer back to Chapter 3 to review technique.

From the ready stance, move your ICG out to your left (figs. 1–2). Now extend your left leg out and behind to your left, into left *nekoashi-dachi* with *hanmi,* covering your body's centerline with both arms (fig. 3). Before planting the foot, execute left *gedan-uke* (low block) with a whipping motion (fig. 4), simultaneously moving through Naifanchi-*dachi* into *zenkutsu-dachi.* Then maneuver through *kakeashi-dachi, musubi-dachi,* and *nekoashi-dachi* as you bring the right foot into *zenkutsu-dachi* and deliver a right whipping punch (figs. 5–8). At the master level, one could place the ICG in front of the waist as one maneuvers

Fig. 9 The body is in *hanmi* in relation to the opponent. This is called *irimi*.

Figs. 10–11 You can move into the opponent's vulnerable spots.

through all these stances from point A to point B. In the process, the body should always be in *hanmi* in relation to the opponent. This is called *irimi*, or the into-body position (fig. 9). This maneuvering creates a non-deadlocked body and allows movement into the opponent's vulnerable spots (figs. 10–11).

Because you are using your ICG, the body does not move up and down as it slides from one point to another. You create the illusion of distance while your body moves closer. In order to place your ICG somewhere other than on your actual CG, your heels will always be lifted slightly from the ground, even in *musubi-dachi*, no matter which direction you move. Some say that it is easy to go forward from *kakeashi-dachi* but hard to reverse the move. However, this is not true, because *kakeashi-dachi* is only a split-second of the whole maneuver. If performed correctly, you can go anywhere from this, or any other, stance. Actually, using the terms "*kakeashi-dachi*" and "*musubi-dachi*" leads to misunderstanding. Naifanchi-*dachi* was the only stance acknowledged by the old masters. Over the course of time, other stances were developed as a teaching tool, but in the process, they have stopped the flow of energy. These so-called modern *tachi* are only tiny parts of the maneuvers, and should never feel like a stance. Because the heels are lifted, the maneuver creates a two-dimensional move to left, right, front, back, or diagonally and a three-dimensional move in the air. You can go anywhere, in any direction, from any stance or position.

This lifted heel is not stable. You must have enough body control to create stability within instability. Unless you are in an unstable condition, you cannot walk, and your energy will be deadlocked (figs. 12–13). This unstable stance is used not only for defense against your opponent's attacks but also for executing your own offensive techniques. This control shows the strength of the martial arts.

Figs. 12–13 This is wrong. Your energy is deadlocked.

Diags. 1–2 Because of the unstable condition, all the energy focused in your ICG goes into your tsuki.

Because of the unstable *kakeashi-dachi*, all the energy focused in your ICG goes into your tsuki and penetrates through the target (diags. 1–2). This unbalanced body is *kyo* and the place of your ICG is *jitsu*. This is the real meaning of attack-counterattack combined. Therefore, learning more and still more different patterns of techniques is useless. The ultimate idea is that as long as the body's energy flows, one strike or one kick will be enough to fight.

The secret of *ken* (fist) is the same as famous Tsukahara Bokuden's (1489–1571 A.D.) "one draw" swordsmanship. If you understand the essence of your craft and have mastered its technique, you will not need several moves to overcome your opponent. You will need only one. This is the martial art that epitomizes Japanese physical culture.

Figs. 1–6 Shift from *zenkutsu-dachi* through *nekoashi-dachi, kakeashi-dachi, musubi-dachi, kakeashi-dachi*, and Naifanchi-*dachi* to *zenkutsu-dachi*.

Figs. 7–9 Straighten your front leg as you extend your waist and ICG toward the back.

Diag. 1 In the movement of a worm, you can find out the essence of Japanese martial arts.

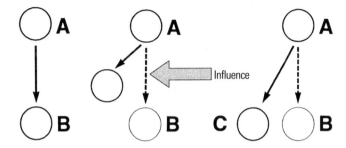

Influence

Diags. 2–4 If the wind blows the object, it will veer off course.

WAIST MOVEMENT

The next maneuver in Taikyoku *Shodan* is to move from point C to point D as you shift from *zenkutsu-dachi* through *nekoashi-dachi*, *kakeashi-dachi*, *musubi-dachi*, *kakeashi-dachi*, and Naifanchi-*dachi* to *zenkutsu-dachi*, facing the opposite direction: seven steps and five different stances (figs. 1–6).

At point C, your front leg straightens as you extend your waist and ICG toward the back (figs. 7–9). Like a worm moving, you shift your ICG toward point D. A worm moves without moving any superficial muscles on its body. Move your center of gravity from chest to waist to legs. Move your sacrum at the same time. Beginners and middle-level practitioners should feel that their center of gravity is at the sacrum. At the master level, you must move the center of gravity to the ICG. Mastery of this technique depends on how to manipulate your CG and ICG. It is too slow to move the waist by rotating it with superficial muscles. As explained earlier, the superior idea of Japanese martial arts is to make a circle with a straight line. Apply this to the wormlike move (diag. 1). So, until you have mastered making a circle with a straight line, study and ponder the worm.

To accomplish this maneuver, you must change your body direction 180 degrees by using a straight line. The concept is the same as you used in executing a straight tsuki without waist rotation. Your ICG is already in front of the opponent, so you just dive into the ICG with a technique. The waist just drops into the ICG, but without rotation. Make sure that this is a straight line. It is difficult to drop the body into the ICG without rotating the waist. Also, if you try to adjust your balance from a rotating move to a straight line, this creates an uneven drop in motion, which interrupts the flow of energy. Picture the Leaning Tower of Pisa. If all goes well, an object dropped from atop the tower will go straight down, falling the shortest distance in the shortest time. But if the wind blows the object, it will veer off course, taking extra time to reach the ground (diags. 2–4).

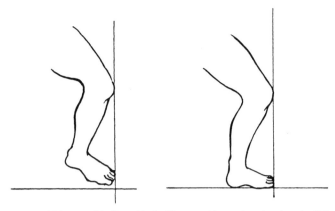

Diags. 5–6 Make a straight line with the big toe and knee, then drop into the ICG.

Figs. 10–12 The secret of swordsmanship. A master swordsman can place a filled saké cup on his calf just behind the knee, swing his sword to the front, and then in the opposite direction, without spilling the saké.

Figs. 13–14 Stand in *kakeashi-dachi*. Without exchanging legs, change direction 180 degrees to the opposite side.

Fig. 1 Tsuki of many traditional Chinese Kung-fu styles.

Fig. 2 If one leans this much against an opponent, he will fall over.

Apply this idea to martial arts, making a straight line with the big toe and knee, then dropping into the ICG while executing a technique (diags. 5–6). The secret of swordsmanship is the same idea. A master swordsman can place a filled saké cup on his calf just behind the knee, swing his sword to the front, then quickly drop the knee, placing his ICG behind him and swinging his sword in the opposite direction, without spilling a drop of the saké (figs. 10–12). Anyone who can achieve this in a split second is indeed a master of swordsmanship. It is only possible to make an efficient circle with a straight line. Those masters of swordsmanship knew the importance of this concept. Muso-Kai uses this method from traditional Okinawan karate. First, stand in *kakeashi-dachi* (fig. 13). Without exchanging legs, change direction 180 degrees to the opposite side, finishing in *kakeashi-dachi* (fig. 14). Even if this motion looks like rotating from another person's point of view, you must feel it as a straight line within the body. That is all there is to it, but with one condition. You must stand not only with lifted heels but you must also shift your ICG from one side to the other without its passing through your body. If the ICG goes inside your body, energy will be momentarily deadlocked within the body. Make sure this move is nice and smooth. Practicing this nearly brings tears of frustration to those higher belts who attempt it. Try it and see how hard this is.

THE MYSTERY OF CHINESE KUNG-FU

Many traditional Chinese Kung-fu styles feature tsuki where the attacker's body is leaning so much that it almost penetrates through the opponent's body (fig. 1). In such a case, if one leans this much against an opponent, he will fall over (fig. 2). However, here we see balance in unbalance, because the energy of the tsuki going

Figs. 3–4 After executing tsuki with one arm, the other arm opens in the opposite direction to create a counterbalance.

Fig. 5 Chinese Kung-fu practitioners of today find their energy deadlocked.

through the target balances the puncher's body. But how does one practice such a technique in katas, where there is no opponent? Chinese Kung-fu incorporates moves where one spreads both arms out wide. The origin for such a technique is that after executing tsuki with one arm, the other arm opens in the opposite direction to create a counterbalance (figs. 3–4). Unfortunately, just as in modern sports karate, Chinese Kung-fu practitioners of today find their energy deadlocked because they have lost the main concept of martial arts, the Imaginary Center of Gravity (fig. 5). They just stand on one leg and open the arms wide without shifting their ICG from its position coincident with their actual center of gravity. They could maintain balance whether both arms were up, one down, or both down. Consider the principle of balance in unbalance: one arm counterbalances the weight of the other. If one arm moves down, the body will lose its balance, and the resulting energy and force are transferred to, and through, the opponent. Traditional Okinawan karate utilizes this type of practice, so it is important to analyze the kata and apply this technique in the right way.

Unfortunately, during the eras of Taisho (1912–1926) and Showa (1926–1989), the climate for cultivating physical culture disappeared. Techniques were lost. Eventually it became impossible to teach this idea to those Japanese who tried to reach world-level body development and even move beyond. This tech-

Fig. 1 *Kokutsu-dachi* is only a split second of motion.   **Fig. 2** This deadlocked position is wrong.

nique came naturally to Gichin Funakoshi, who created the Taikyoku katas, so he simply demonstrated the movement to karate students, and saved the thousand words needed to create the proverbial picture. However, without a verbal explanation, few if any karateka could understand what he was showing them.

There was some idea about body control in Western culture before the eighteenth century. Then James Watt (1736–1819) invented the steam engine, which began the Industrial Revolution. Because this engine could produce hundreds, even thousands, of times the power of a human being, we no longer needed the body's natural efficiency, and physical culture lost its importance. Japan followed the path of the West, and katas declined in importance. They were viewed as relics of the past, okay to keep as a sport for competition or for historical value, but having no real value for the modern student. As machines took over jobs formerly performed by the human body, man forgot how his body had once functioned. Eventually the body was no longer capable of its past achievements and the need for katas was forgotten as well. But traditional Okinawan katas offer much more than that. They hold the essence of real fighting.

MAROBOSHI

Kokutsu-dachi is used often in modern karate, but not in traditional Okinawan karate. It is a stance which extends the front leg forward while bending the back knee and putting one's weight on the back leg. This stance creates a deadlocked position because the center of gravity shifts through the center of the body as it moves from point C to point D. This stance was made when karate was introduced to Japan. Actually, in present-day Okinawan karate, there is no such thing as *kokutsu-dachi*. It is only a split second of the motion of moving the body like a worm to shift the body's position. Therefore, it does not look powerful. The so-called *kokutsu-dachi* of today has become even more deadlocked, following efforts to make it look showy (figs. 1–2). A practical kata does not look fancy. A practical kata, as seen in traditional karate, maneuvers so smoothly that the motion is never stopped by delivery of techniques. The move is finished before one realizes it has begun. Compare this to modern kata which call for a wide stance before execution of techniques, with each movement frozen for a moment, so all can see. Instructors who can teach traditional kata are able to see the frame-by-frame movement within continuous movement. They can "see" the ICG, not with the naked eye, but with *kan-no-me* (diag. 1). Therefore, you must heed the old saying, "Find a good master, even if it takes more than three years."

Taikyoku *Shodan* is the first and easiest kata. Even so, depending on how you count, there are six to eight "stances" within each of some twenty moves from one point to another. As you learn how to place your ICG, *kyo*, and *jitsu*, and to see with *kan-no-me*, this easy kata becomes a master level kata.

Diag. 1 They can "see" the ICG with *kan-no-me*.

The last stage of learning kata is to anticipate the opponent's reaction and use it against him. When you execute a punch with ICG and the opponent blocks it, you then use the reaction energy from blocking to execute your next technique while consciously shifting your ICG. This is different from a modern-day combination. In a split second, you read the reaction of the opponent. Instantaneously, you shift your ICG and deliver a technique to your opponent's vulnerable spot. At first, the opponent's body leads the fight. Before long, his body switches to following your strategy. You use *kyo-jitsu* to make the switch. Allow the opponent to execute a technique to *kyo*, which his eyes tell him is the target. Before his technique reaches *kyo* (where he believes your body is), move your ICG to his deadlocked body and deliver your technique. This is the secret move that is called *maroboshi* in Shinkage-ryu swordsmanship. Your body becomes like a huge rock rolling down the hill, never stopping, gathering more energy with each revolution. This is the idea of traditional kata. Therefore, mastering this move applies to a real fight. In this way, even the simple Taikyoku Shodan kata can take two or three years to master. Practice makes all the difference. There is no practical use for today's "fancy" katas that move from point A to point B, but deadlock the performer's energy along the way. What counts is not how many katas one knows, but

Figs. 3–4 At the beginner level, one practices the concept of ICG, but at the middle level, the upper and lower body move in different directions.

Figs. 5–6 You are learning to manipulate *kyo-jitsu* and maneuver by bending the body.

knowing one kata with *kan-no-me*. If you fully master one, you understand all. The old masters always said, "Do not trust practitioners who are proud of the number of katas they know." Complete mastery of kata means an observer will think that your kata is only like walking.

At the beginner level one practices the concept of Imaginary Center of Gravity. The middle level is different. At this level, the upper and lower body move in different directions (figs. 3–4). Here you are learning to manipulate *kyo-jitsu* and maneuver by bending the body (figs. 5–6). In Okinawan traditional dance, there is a technique to control the maneuver, dazzling the three-dimensional sense. There is a saying in Okinawan karate, "An essential idea of karate is seen

Fig. 7 This willowlike bending of the body, in Okinawan traditional dance, is the key to body control.

in women's dance." This willowlike bending of the body is the key to body control (fig. 7).

This does not mean that the hand motions from this dance can be used as strikes and throws. If that is the importance of karate, then Okinawan karate is only a second-class martial art, and only a collection of thousands of hand and leg techniques. The Naifanchi of Choki Motobu is as follows. First, simply tilt the body forward, damming your energy against gravity's fall. Next, without showing the opponent, bend the body to disguise the distance between the two of you. Last, simply walk to produce the energy. This is the level of Ueshiba's Aikido that claims walking is the technique. Chibana had *kan-no-me* to comprehend this walking. But even in his generation, there were few who had *kan-no-me*. Even his direct pupils did not understand the essence of karate. This is the reason that the masters disliked showing their katas to people from other styles of karate. This is the limitation of attempting to pass the essence of karate from one person to another. A master can point out the existence of *kan-no-me*, but discovering and mastering it is all up to the effort and talent of the student. In other words, if one has talent for martial arts, one can see and understand from words or from one picture. Final enlightenment cannot be learned from the instructor, but can only be realized by the student himself when he finally achieves understanding.

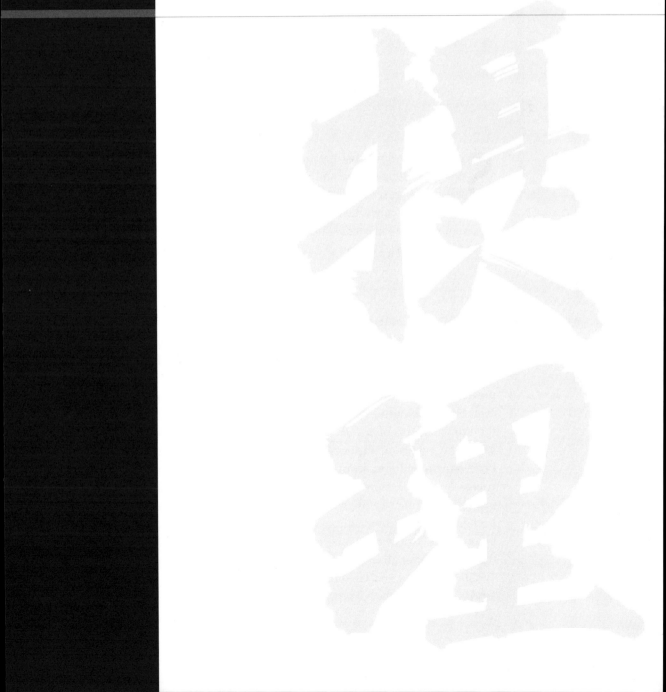

THE DIVINE PROVIDENCE OF THE UNIVERSE

Chapter 6

The Eternal Truth of All

Since ancient times, martial arts masters have been able to sense a murderous foe lurking unseen and intent upon attack. In other words, these masters could sense *sakki*: the *ki* of the kill, a blood thirst in another human being. Today you might hear of a master throwing someone without touching that opponent. The master is said to have used an invisible *ki* to throw his foe. This *ki* is an intrinsic element of Eastern body control. What is this mysterious *ki*?

KI

From China comes the concept we call *ki* in martial arts. Sometimes this notion of *ki* is mixed with the soul, or spiritual belief. In today's martial arts world, everyone thinks *ki* can force an opponent down with no physical contact, or enable one to sense an opponent's thoughts. *Ki* is perceived as being a mystical power. Japanese martial arts view *ki* as a practical, even a philosophical concept, but not a mystical one. The Japanese language has many different words for different forms of *ki*. *Kaki* is the *ki* for the energy of combustion. *Jyoki* is the *ki* for the energy of vaporization. *Aiki* is the *ki* for the combined energies between you and your opponent. In old China, *ki* (or *chi* in Chinese) meant energy in general. Now *ki* is thought of in a more imprecise way. In today's martial arts world, we often use *ki* as a sales pitch, and little more. There has been no scientific observation, no attempt to analyze and understand this mysterious force. However, Japanese culture always took a more pragmatic view of this energy. After all, the concept of *bu* in budo includes systematic thinking. Traditional karate and Japanese swordsmanship never stressed the mysterious aspects of *ki* when they discussed it.

Diag. 1 It is possible to use *ki* to read someone's body language.

INVESTIGATION OF *KI*

Reading Body Language

It is possible to use *ki* to guess someone's intentions from his body movements, or body language. With a mastery of *ki*, one could read another's subconscious mind (diag. 1). You have heard of married couples who are able to read each other's thoughts, not because of psychic abilities, but because each knows the other so well that he or she anticipates the other's thoughts from their actions. The Kanji characters for the Japanese words *kehai* (気配, awareness of surroundings and circumstances) and *kikubari* (気配り, sensitivity to people's needs) are the same. Using *ki* to read the world around you will make you more sensitive to all aspects of your surroundings. *Sakki* indicates the opposite sensitivity: an awareness of danger. *Kishoku* indicates an uneasiness in the presence of an object or another person. Dogs, cats, and other animals use these forms of *ki* to survive in the wild.

Using All Your Senses

A second source of *ki*, which you may never have considered, is the combination of the five senses which you have used since birth to learn more about your surroundings. The senses of smell and taste lead us to food, or away from unpleasant odors. Hearing and vision enable us to gather information from books, television, and other people. The sense of touch is one of the most important to a small child just beginning to explore his world. The so-called sixth sense is not so easily defined. It takes one or more of the familiar five and adds individual judgment. Because we have used these five senses all of our lives, we can tabulate a conclusion based on personal experience, then use our minds to formulate a qualified judgment about our current situation. The resulting reaction is fueled by the combined energies of experience and rational thought. This is a partial example of the *ki* indicated by *kehai, kishoku, kikubari,* and *sakki*.

Ki as an Electrical Force

Let's look at a third possibility for explaining *ki*. Does *ki* act like a radio wave? Is it matter smaller than atoms in a magnetic field? Is it an electrical wave or impulse traveling through space, which can push or throw an object upon contact? Some karate practitioners today believe *ki* is an unknown wave produced by the brain and transmitted throughout the body, and that this wave can travel through space to attack a target without physical contact. Although science does not yet understand *ki*, it is beginning to acknowledge its existence. The Large Hadron Collider project in Europe will examine proton-proton collisions at previously unreachable speeds, and has the potential to prove the existence of a fifth dimension. Could this fifth dimension be *ki*?

The ancients thought that all matter in the universe could be reduced to four elements: earth, water, air, and fire. Today we know that these substances are composites of smaller atoms and subatomic particles. Physicists recognize four fundamental forces holding these particles together. These four forces are: gravity, electromagnetism, strong (nuclear force which powers our sun and the stars), and weak (force responsible for radioactive decay). The human body is only able to harness the force of gravity. As scientists unlocked the mysteries of each of these forces, the course of civilization changed forever. The Theory of Everything is science's quest to unite these four into one super force. The Superstring theory currently holds the most promise to unite Einstein's theory of relativity and the theory of quantum physics in explaining all physical knowledge. This Superstring theory assumes the existence of a ten-dimensional universe.

Dr. Shigemi Sasaki, a Tokai University professor, believes *ki* is a very real force, not a mysterious philosophy. He is a member of the Japan Technology Transfer Association, which is conducting an experiment that spins both positive and negative poles of a huge magnet. This will create an area of neutral energy midway between the poles. This is called the "*ki* space" which collects *ki* energy. If this project succeeds, *ki* will no longer be mysterious matter. However, even if mankind is able to elucidate *ki*, its tiny amount of energy must still rely on transfer through some medium in order to reach the target. The principle of transferring this type of energy is the same as sending an electrical wave through the artificial medium of television or radio in order to transmit picture and sound. It seems impossible to use the human body as this medium.

Let's assume for a moment that *ki* is an energy force similar to a radio wave and is stronger than the *ki* which uses the senses or reads body language. We will perform a scientific experiment. Blindfold two people. If *ki* is indeed this form of viable energy source, one person should be able to push or throw his opponent, without either actually touching the other, simply by exerting this energy. I think that your experiment will fail.

To continue with our deductions, can *ki* be produced in an open space by reading body language? If this is so, it must exist in both you and your opponent in order to receive or send it. If *ki* is in the flow of air, the brain can process information gathered from all the body's senses and respond appropriately. If this is the case, a martial artist could harness this form of *ki*. First, use *kihaku* (the *ki* of determination and commitment) to place your ICG far behind your opponent. Your leaning forward to accomplish this will weaken your opponent by forcing his ICG to also move behind him. Just as with the box in Chapter 2, his weight has been moved off his balance point. But this does not mean that the power of your *ki* has pushed your opponent's body back. Your opponent has unconsciously moved back to avoid the attack that your body language told him was imminent.

"Suppress *ki* to knock out the opponent" means to execute techniques without showing fighting spirit. Without communicating anything from your body language, place your ICG on your opponent and execute your chosen techniques. Some people seem to view *ki* as having the aspect of pushing or throwing an object or person. *Ki* is not something that can be snatched from the air and hurled at an opponent. Rather, by using a combination of body language and the senses, a martial artist must consciously or unconsciously create *ki* to control the opponent. You have the advantage of using your uncooperative opponent's force against him as part of the power of your *ki*.

DEADLOCKED CULTURE

Many people today look at *ki* as a mysterious entity and as a romantic mystique of martial arts. In particular, some so-called martial artists who have not understood the essence of karate have interpreted *ki* as a mystical force. It was different long ago. Japanese swordsmen of old, who experienced real life and death fighting, understood *ki* as the *kyo* and *jitsu* of gravitational force. This is not saying, however, that the essence of swordsmanship is *ki*. For old-time Chinese martial artists, *ki* was the whole of energy and was used in their daily life.

China has an interesting history. Their peak development of thought and technology occurred over two thousand years ago during the Warring States Period (403–221 B.C.). This era has ever since been revered as a heritage, with no attempts to improve upon or surpass it. This is the historical stagnation that Hegel described in his *Philosophy of History*. If Chinese science had progressed after the Warring States Period, they could have avoided the stagnation of Confucianism. This *ki* that was described as the whole energy would have been studied more, and we would now have formulas to describe it, just as we do for the universal laws of gravity or Archimedes' principle of the displacement of matter. The energy of *ki* could have been developed and harnessed, just as Watt harnessed steam for his steam engine.

This was paralleled in Chinese medicine. Eastern medicine is now being reconsidered because of the side effects of so many Western drugs. But Chinese medicine's development has stagnated since the sixteenth century, especially in the fields of bacteriology, surgery, and genetics. The technical aspects of acupuncture and acupressure have been passed on, but no one has developed and explored them scientifically so that everyone can understand how these aid the flow of *ki* in the body.

In the way that the Chinese describe *ki*, the ICG (which uses gravity's force) is also *ki*. If this is *ki*, then the ICG is not a mystery. The *ki* of karate is not an electrical wave or atomic particles that shoot out of the brain to overtake and defeat an opponent. Nor is it a wave approaching from the opponent's brain, which you can see and thus read his next move. The *ki* of martial arts is the unconscious mind which reaches into the opponent's mind and concludes his next move by reading his body language and gathering all available information from the five senses. The *ki* of martial arts is the conscious mind that processes all this information and attacks by controlling gravity's force.

Since Pavlov's dog experiments, many studies have proven the correlation between the senses and the conscious and unconscious mind. Mankind has enough knowledge and technology to explain *ki*. All martial arts must consider analyzing *ki* on a scientific basis. Otherwise this marvelous heritage from Eastern martial arts body control will be lost forever. Without action, martial arts will be ruined by Western sports-based karate which only works based on pure physical speed and muscle power and does not rely on the universal laws.

DIFFICULTY OF MARTIAL ARTS

Putting *ki* on your fist as you strike means executing your technique with concentration and fighting spirit. That fighting spirit causes your opponent to feel intimidated and shrink back. This shrinking causes your ICG to move to his actual center of gravity and deadlocks your opponent's energy.

You must consider this, though. Whether you execute techniques with suppressed *ki* or full *ki*, the physical condition will be the same. That is, the ICG will be outside your body between you and your opponent, and you must know, with a calm mind, where to place the ICG. This is the highest level of martial arts as physical culture. Some practitioners concentrate only on the theory and forget about physical development; others work only on muscle and speed and forget about the theory; both lose speed and power as they grow older (diag. 1). Martial arts students must therefore use the brain to understand the theory and use the body to apply the theory to real life practice.

That leads us to one more concept to make you a complete martial artist. This is *Shinpo*, mind control.

Diag. 1 If you concentrate only on theory, or work only on muscle and speed, you will lose speed and power as you grow older.

SHINPO

There are two facets of mastering *shinpo* in Japanese martial arts. One is to control your mind; the other is to control your opponent's mind. This is the mind of calmness, or serenity. Martial artists of old tried to master this calmness by practicing Zen meditation atop a high mountain or under a waterfall. Every

Diag. 1 Morihei Ueshiba was able to see himself in a fight with a "universal eye."

martial artist hopes to cut himself off from *Bon-no* (Buddhism's 108 struggles or stresses of life) and bring out his most serene self at any time.

In the game of *Go*, there is the term *okame-hachimoku*. *Oka* means the impartial third person, who is able to keep eight steps ahead of the players because of his ability to view the whole of a situation. In other words, it is better to see a situation from the third person's point of view. The secret of martial arts is to become this *oka*. Even when one is fighting with an opponent, he puts himself outside the fight to observe the fight. This way he can see the ICG between himself and the opponent and spontaneously anticipate the next placement for ICG.

Aikido uses this concept to execute techniques. The ultimate goal of Aikido is not just to match the opponent's *ki*, but also to observe the fight from the universal point of view that is called "becoming one with the universe." Ueshiba passed down to his students his understanding of this "universal eye" which can observe oneself in one's surroundings (diag. 1). This does not necessarily mean that, just because Ueshiba understood this principle of the universal eye, all Aikido practitioners then and now have understood it.

Martial arts could be called the idea of "one." It is up to you, the individual, to incorporate your personal ideas and experiences into your understanding and ultimate mastery of the martial arts, and further, of your life. One's personal experiences and perceptions cannot be transferred to another person. No matter how good your teacher is, in the end it is up to you to apply everything you have learned to your body, your abilities, and your situation. You must discover a way that not only works for you but is you.

At Muso-Kai Okinawa Karate-do, we practice traditional katas. We also sponsor sport-based tournaments, with competition in kata, *koshiki* (sparring while wearing protective gear), and full-contact fighting (figs. 1–3). Of course, in a life

Figs. 1–3 Muso-Kai's sport-based tournaments, with competitions in kata, *koshiki*, and full-contact fighting.

and death fight, there are no rules. You might say that it is not possible to learn the essence of martial arts through a tournament. This is true, but today's world does not permit the life and death fights of old. Therefore, today's tournament arena is the only venue for experiencing martial arts and experimenting with the universal laws. Here, within this condensed moment of quasi-reality, one can find a bit of the romance, mystique, and excitement of yesterday's martial arts. Karate study must include tournament participation as well as kata.

MUSO-KAI KARATE

Chapter 7

Karate That Enriches Life

It should now be clear that traditional Okinawan karate and modern karate are completely different from each other. Why is there so much difference between these two? The time and place that karate was introduced to Japan caused the difference. It was a time when Japan was open to receiving new knowledge from all over the world. New generations of high school and college students were studying the philosophies of Descartes, Schopenhauer, and Kant. These young people viewed karate as an old-fashioned, nationalistic practice. What foreign karate they did study from Okinawa was explained by Western sports methods. There were, of course, still some who remembered the body control techniques of Japanese *ken-jutsu* and *ju-jutsu* from the Edo era (1600–1868). Some students tried to understand Okinawan karate by applying those Japanese martial arts basics.

Unfortunately, due to the overwhelming influence of Western sports culture after World War II, traditional karate was nearly destroyed after 1945. With modern technology and karate's growing popularity came a misunderstanding of the underlying principles of martial arts. The universal laws and harnessing of gravity were abandoned in pursuit of punches and kicks which looked stronger and faster, but actually were not, because they had lost touch with the essence utilized by the early masters.

When karate became a sport, it became much easier for American and European cultures to participate and practice. Western cultures were intrigued to learn the secrets of a formerly closed martial society. Its mixture of well-organized discipline and authentic Eastern manners caught the hearts of Western people. Even today in Japan, many parents send their children to a dojo because they believe it is a good place to learn manners and discipline.

When you look back through history, you can see that it was inevitable that karate would be embraced first as exotic, then as a sport, by the Western world. But we do not recognize and study karate today simply because it has gained world popularity. Karate is not just a form of exercise or a passing fad. The study of martial arts has much to teach us about ourselves and about life.

THE PURPOSE OF MARTIAL ARTS TODAY

It is taboo to say "if" in history. No matter how much we may mourn the loss of the old masters' teachings, there is no way mankind could have prevented the changes brought about in martial arts as the rest of the world changed. That is why I have written this book: to use as a guide for the future, so we can avoid making the same mistakes again. *Kyo* and *jitsu* may seem to have no relevance in today's world. However, understanding the true meaning of *kyo* and *jitsu* still applies to modern times. To paraphrase Kant in his *Critique of Pure Reason*, change only occurs in phenomena (facts or events, the world of experience), not in the noumena (the eternal, intangible world). In other words, your surroundings or circumstances may change, but the essence, or identity, remains the same. This is the true meaning and purpose of philosophical existence (identity), and karate is the identity that the martial arts comprehended in theory and practice seven hundred years ago. This is the foundation of martial arts that was the ultimate of physical culture in Japan. Thus karate has the ability to contribute to human society as a culture.

In other words, martial artists have understood Newton's laws and applied them along with theoretical physics, such as *Shinpo*'s mind control, to the development of the human body. This means that in human history, compared to technology, physical culture has already been completed. There is a limit to Hegel's philosophy. He believed that his time was the high point of the development of the total human being. The human body and mind do not advance in the same manner that technology does. Humans still have only two arms, two legs, and one brain with which to perform all actions. Unless this basic design could be improved upon, the ultimate performance of the human body has been realized by the old martial arts masters. Their knowledge was all-encompassing. Because of progress in the fields of science and technology, our methods of explaining and applying their essential concepts have changed, but the essence itself has been there since the days of the old masters. The essence of tragedy and comedy in literature was consummated in the Greek era. Plato and Socrates discussed the essence of politics and philosophy. In Eastern culture, the essence of thought was reached during the Spring and Fall Period (B.C. 770–403) and the Warring State Period (B.C. 403–221) in China. The existence of knowledge or thought between the conscious and unconscious mind that we are studying in modern science already existed in Japanese martial arts, though without today's technical terminology. The concepts are the same, whether or not you use modern terminology to explain them.

For example, Zen Master Takuan (1573–1645 A.D.) said during the early Edo era, "It is the very mind itself/That leads the mind astray; /Of the mind, /Do not be mindless." (from *The Unfettered Mind*, translated by William Scott Wilson, Kodansha International, 1986). The so-called ultimate mind control of modern sports psychology utilizes the same idea Master Takuan passed on to his followers.

We must constantly create a modern interpretation of the pure, traditional essence of Okinawan karate. It is as Michel Foucault explained when he found the Chinese encyclopedia, that everything is changed when one looks at it a different way. One's perspective and preconceived notions alter one's perception. One must use the concept of *kan-no-me* to fully comprehend the principles of the martial arts put forth in this book and to apply them not only to karate, but also to harmonizing one's life with the lives of others and, indeed, with the whole of the world and the universe. To achieve balance in unbalance, one must view the world not just from an Eastern perspective or from a Western perspective, but with a universal point of view. Do we aim too high if we say an understanding of theoretical physics is as natural to the martial arts as *kan-no-me*? We are in a unique position to apply these theoretical ideas to the real world and demonstrate them within our own bodies.

PHYSICAL AND MIND CULTURE IN A TECHNOLOGICAL CIVILIZATION

Masters of the martial arts experience and express the laws of the universe. They are the ones who can see Newton's law of motion when performing body maneuvers. An ordinary man can only see a thrown object going up, but one who has *kan-no-me* is able to see the gravitational force which will pull it down. For example, if you throw a ball to a two-year-old baby, the baby will try to catch the ball at the height he first sees it. But as the baby grows up, he is able to see the gravitational force on the ball and thus predict its landing point (diag. 1). Martial arts experts are able to see and use this force in daily life and

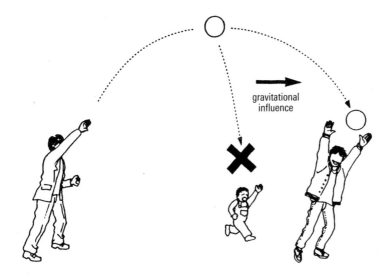

Diag. 1 As the baby grows up, he is able to see the gravitational force on the ball and thus predict its landing point.

understand that all motion is influenced by this force. They can consciously control gravity's force, moving against gravity or using it to accelerate.

There are paintings in India showing ascetics who are experiencing Yoga. Some are floating in the air; some are portrayed with a third eye on the forehead. These pictures were painted by people who understood *kyo* and *jitsu*. The body which stays on the ground is *kyo*, the physical shell without spirit and, therefore, incomplete. *Jitsu* is the real body, complete with spirit, which floats. And the third eye is observing the world, *kan-no-me*. It is useless to try to lift up a body and actually float as in the picture. It is foolish to imprint a tattoo on the forehead. The painter is drawing a concept, using the human body as an example. It should be obvious to martial artists or religious people that these are only representations of *kyo* and *jitsu*. It only matters that one understand the concept, not whether one actually has a third eye or is floating in air.

Even if a person is blind, with *kan-no-me* he can observe the world better than with normal eyesight. Since the Meiji era (1868–1912 A.D.), the Japanese martial arts which have truly understood *kyo* and *jitsu* have dramatically decreased. Without a true understanding of *jitsu* one cannot create *kyo*. Without being able to observe *kyo*, one cannot see *jitsu*.

Most of what is written about Japanese martial arts at a worldwide level treats it as a sport. What little explanation there is exists only as translations of publications written in Japan. A good example is seen in the MBA program at Harvard University, which used *The Book of Five Rings* by Miyamoto Musashi as a text for its business school. They used this book because they valued the unusual economic development of Japan and tried to understand it from an old publication. However, unless they understand *kan-no-me* and use it to observe the economic world, they do not understand the Japanese economy. Therefore, they glorify only the morality or formality which is a characteristic of martial arts, or take up only the mysterious *ki* which satisfies a yen for mysticism.

From the spiritual side, many who long for Zen are only attracted by its mystique or are dissatisfied by Christianity. They never fully understand it or convert to it.

Worst of all, the Japanese, whose heritage is this physical culture, are losing this ability to see with *kan-no-me*. If the Japanese martial arts are to raise the stature of their culture among the world, they must have a solid understanding of their own culture. Their old martial artist ancestors had this solid understanding and applied the use of universal gravity in their daily life. Likely, they already sensed in their own way and applied the principles of Einstein's law of relativity. They were able to see beyond time and place to a higher understanding of their universe.

The Buddhist monk Kukai (774–835 A.D.) fasted and meditated while the planet Venus rose on the horizon, until he eventually "swallowed" Venus; that is, he felt its essence become part of him. Tibetan monks spend many hours, even days, creating an intricate mandala (ritual sand painting), then destroy it. This is to illustrate that it is not the act of creating that is meaningful, but rather understanding what it represents.

SEE THE WORLD WITH *KAN-NO-ME*

What is the universal attraction that Japanese or Eastern culture holds? And how can this insight be shared with the world? *Kan-no-me* is applicable not only to karate, but also to all of life, even stationary objects. In Western culture, whoever has *kan-no-me* has a creative mind and is able to produce something original because of it.

Frank Lloyd Wright (1867–1959 A.D.) is a good example. One of his most famous architectural designs, Fallingwater, is a good example of *kan-no-me* (fig. 1). His vision of what no one else could see created the perfect symbiotic relationship between structure and landscape. This house has become one with the landscape. Most of the time, artistically talented architects clash with structural engineers, because their artistic ideas do not conform with gravity's effects on the structure. If an ordinary architect designs a home at the edge of a cliff, he will place it near the edge of the cliff. This is creating by avoiding gravity. A talented architect will extend part of the house beyond the cliff's edge, supporting it with walls or struts from below. This is creating against gravity. But Frank Lloyd Wright was different. He placed the house in perfect balance with the

Fig. 1 Frank Lloyd Wright's architectural design Fallingwater at Bear Run, Pennsylvania.

Fig. 2 *David*, marble statue by Michelangelo.

waterfall, part on the ground and part over the water, without a need for additional supports. This is balance in unbalance. Before Wright studied architecture, he studied physics, so he knew the relationship of the universal laws to buildings. He loved small hills and built houses on such sites. But he built his houses partway up the hill, never on top of the hill, because that would change the character of the hill. He understood balance in unbalance; he understood the need for a coexistence between nature and the artificial object.

Michelangelo (1475–1564 A.D.), the famous sculptor, created many works using the very difficult medium of marble. Artists and laymen alike were amazed at his skill in studying the marble, then beginning to chisel the stone without first drawing lines on the stone. "I just chisel the object out of the marble," he said. He instinctively saw the figure within the marble, waiting to be released from the stone (fig. 2).

Someone praising Japanese calligraphy would say, "There is flow in the stroke," or "The stroke has force." Because the hand holding the brush just follows the Imaginary Center of Gravity, the stroke retains vitality and is never deadlocked.

On a trip to Japan, I visited my sister. She took me to a pottery museum near her home. She asked me to pick out three or so pieces that I liked. I chose three. When she checked in a pamphlet to see who had made them, she was amazed to learn they were all made by a master artist of pottery. I had instinctively recognized pottery which retained the energy of its creation.

It is the same in music. Listening to a classic piano recital, one especially notices the flow. If a pianist makes a mistake, for a split second he notices it and is distracted, even if most of the audience is unaware and the piece ends smoothly. One who has *kan-no-me* is able to sense that split second of deadlocked energy.

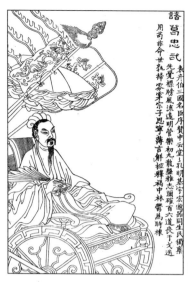

Diag. 1 An illustration of General Zhuge Liang.

MARTIAL ARTS AS *HYOHO*

Long ago, this *kan-no-me* was used in many areas: politics, economics, the military, and anything that related to human living. This was called *Hyoho* or *Heiho*, the strategy. The *Romance of Three Kingdoms*, a history attributed to Luo Guanzhang (Lo Kuan-Chung, 330–400 A.D.), tells of the great master of *Hyoho*, General Zhuge Liang (Chu ko Liang, 181–234 A.D.), who was able to read the enemy's *ki* (diag. 1). This prime minister of Shu could anticipate his enemies' military moves, just as we read our opponent's body language and anticipate his next move in martial arts. He could see their ICG going behind them if they were scared, or moving to the front if they were determined to win or die in battle. He used the force of ICG to become a brilliant strategist.

Okinawan karate only embodies those physical laws which apply 100 percent efficiency to human movement. In other words, it is more efficient to rely on the universal forces instead of one's own physical strength. We find this same idea of an appreciation of the universe in the world's religions. Another way of saying this is "to become one with the universe."

We humans may think of ourselves as the most important living things ever created, but the human being is only one of many life forms that are allowed to inhabit this universe. From the universal point of view, you and your opponent fighting each other are only two living things among many. Understanding this idea will change your point of view and give a different direction to your life from all existing thoughts, ideas, and philosophies. The martial arts that were born in life and death fighting will become a tool for peace. This is the way that *Hyoho*, strategy, became *Heiho*, the way of peace. Perhaps Japan's gift to world culture is this *shinshin bunka*, spirit and body enlightenment. Among traditional Japanese martial arts, Muso-Kai Okinawa Karate-do is able to provide the essence of the universe. It is up to the readers of this book to understand this idea and use these techniques to bring true peace to the twenty-first century.

ACKNOWLEDGMENT

I would like to acknowledge the following people for their help in bringing this book to martial artists throughout the world. First, thanks must go to my black belt student, Munenori Yamamoto, for his initial work on translating my book from Japanese to English. Kathleen Ivey, a fourth degree black belt student, was invaluable in researching and checking my terminology, and refining the translation. I also thank Debra Henderson for her assistance in editing and polishing the translation. This book would not be possible without their combined efforts.

Arsen Mkrtchyan, a black belt in Muso-Kai karate, was a model in many of the photographs in this book. His patience and dedication to the art of karate deserve recognition. Ikuo Kanemura, editor of the Japanese version, was everything an editor should be. He believed in me and truly went the extra mile to get me published. Tetsuo Kuramochi, senior editorial director of Kodansha International, was instrumental in bringing this book to readers worldwide.

Finally, I wish to thank all the instructors and masters who shared their time and knowledge with me over the last thirty-five years. Because of them, we are all standing on the shoulders of giants.

INDEX